UNKNOWING & ASTONISHMENT

Meditations on Faith for the Long Haul

Christopher Scott

SLG Press
Convent of the Incarnation
Fairacres, Parker Street
Oxford OX4 1TB
www.slgpress.co.uk

ISBN 978-0-7283-0298-3
ISSN 0307-1405

Cover image: Ikon of Christ the Saviour by Andrei Rublev, *c.*1410, in the Tretyakov Gallery, Moscow.

Printed by
Short Run Press Ltd, Exeter

For Linda
and for our fellow travellers
David, Michael & Clare
and their families

Preface

This small book started life as a project paper for a Clergy Course at St George's House, Windsor, in 2003. I am very grateful to St George's for agreeing to its publication and giving their blessing in this respect. I also would like to thank Canon John White for his support and encouragement in the development of these pages.

I was really set on this journey following a meeting in 1985 with the late Hugh Kay, at the time editor of *The Month*, who encouraged me to write an article where the parish priest asks himself 'How do I set about evangelising people without misleading them into thinking that faith is mostly a matter of certainty and comfort? How do I tell them that faith is often a life that must be lived in the dark, without being destructive of simple belief?' It was published in 1985 titled, 'The Uncertainty of Faith'.

Equally, the contents of this short work have been coloured by the commonplace book I have maintained since 1973. Here I recorded passages from theological and other writings that seemed to me to have a particular relevance for the churches in these times as we engage with the mystery of faith. Inevitably, perhaps, certain prominent themes began to emerge which I have attempted to explore with greater transparency. Alongside my own contribution, some of the quotations recorded in the following chapters act as a mini-anthology that underpin the main theme.

Since 1982 I have also been closely associated with the contemplative Community of the Servants of the Will of God at Crawley Down Monastery in West Sussex, which has offered me a sense of direction and a new appreciation of tradition for which I am evergrateful. My gratitude is also due to SLG Press for offering to publish this book.

Christopher Scott
Bude, July 2017

CONTENTS

INTRODUCTION

St Augustine wrote: 'God is closer to us than we are to ourselves.'[1] This serves as a theme for the cameos and vignettes on the nature of faith contained in this book. It immediately suggests for all of us who have been nurtured in the faith (whether superficially or with more rigour) that a new attention is needed to what may have been stirred up within us. For this is the God whom Christ reveals to us—not a distant and far away God who winds up the universe like a mechanical clock and then leaves it to tick away under its own steam.

There is, I believe, a fine distinction to be made between *knowing about* religious truths and *actually knowing* you have been addressed by a presence which comes from you-know-not-quite-where, but yet is unmistakable in the mark it leaves upon you.

The essential premise of this book is that to encounter the Christian faith is to enter a new world. This encounter is embraced by a willing surrender to the call of faith, and a subsequent unfolding of a new vision of the world we inhabit. A recurring theme is the way in which faith finds vital expression in the desert tradition, whereby it is frequently experienced as an 'unknowing' before it is a knowing of God. Here I seek to encourage confidence in the distinctive character and traditions of the Church's spiritual life. These pages begin and conclude with the sacramental experience of worship, not as an auxiliary component in Christian living, but as the active heart of God's new creation which is descending into our midst.

In effect, every Christian is called in some sense to be a theologian—that is, one whose life and purpose is grounded in the being and love of God. 'In God we live and move and have our being' (Acts 17:28). Evagrius of Pontus underlines the point: 'If you pray truly you are a theologian.'[2]

The truth is that because of our blindness, our hardness of heart and our inner fears and reservations, we do not live as if this were the case. Once the first flush of enthusiasm in Christian believing has faded, we need a theology that is adequate for the long haul, and which continues to unfold and illuminate our experience of life even in times of aridity or when God is seemingly absent. Yet, too easily we avoid this tension, adept as we are at domesticating the things of God.

Out of the questions that are addressed in these pages, it is my concern to reignite a sense of delight and hope where faith is eclipsed either by self-seeking materialism or by militant fundamentalism, or indeed by sheer weariness from a jaded spirituality. Religious language tells a story, and like any other language we have to learn it—it is an overarching parable which points to depths of meaning we so easily avoid in life, and it is a story that has its footprints planted firmly in history.

[1] *The Confessions of St Augustine*, Book 1 (London: Fontana, 1963), 31.

[2] Evagrius of Pontus (ascetical and mystical writer, monk of Sketis in Egypt 346–399), *Treatise on Prayer*, quoted in Bishop Kallistos Ware, *The Orthodox Way* (New York: SVS Press, 1996), 61.

I

GATES OF MYSTERY

> The image or icon is part of a whole approach to theology, an approach that sees theology as illuminating the journey of the Christian into God, rather than some speculative enterprise.
>
> *Andrew Louth* [1]

THERE happen in our lives certain moments which stand out from the normal ebb and flow of daily existence. It is as if a different order of things comes into play, lifting us up to a new place. In 1993 the Victoria and Albert Museum in London hosted an exquisite exhibition, *Gates of Mystery: the art of Holy Russia.* Here were gathered some of the finest surviving examples of Russian medieval art, many of the icons having been rescued by the State Museum during the political turmoil of the twentieth century in Russia.

The exhibition ran until the end of the year, and idly I kept saying to my wife that we must go and see it. Four days before Christmas, I realised I was going to miss it. Uncharacteristically for a clergyman at this time of year, I had a free afternoon, and on the spur of the moment leapt into the car and drove the hour straight up to South Kensington. A vacant parking place awaited me right opposite the museum.

I was quite unprepared for the experience that greeted me as I entered the exhibition. The icons were breathtaking in their range and quality, and in the strength and subtlety of their colours. We are used to seeing icons as pictures in books or small reproductions on a study wall, but some of them were vast—literally the size of doors—gates of mystery into heaven.

What impressed me, equally, was the hushed atmosphere that greeted these treasures. Somewhere in the background there echoed the resonant sound of a Russian choir—almost a whisper. The milieu was more reverential than a church. People just stood there—still, gazing, attentive—almost oblivious to anything else. I have never forgotten those two hours on a winter's afternoon. It was as if these icons were speaking to us from another world. As I continue to reflect on this memory, many years later, it would not be fanciful to say that there, in that place, at that time, were 'the angels of God ascending and descending upon the Son of Man' (John 1:51)

Yet too much religious-speak in our times is quite disconnected from our human situation. How can we know God, when we do not even know ourselves? How does this Son of Man upon whom the angels descend, relate to our own faltering awareness of our humanity. Alternatively, the pedlars of quick-fix religion saddle their followers with institutional or psychological baggage that all too easily dulls the soul, inhibits the imagination, and domesticates God, effectively cutting God down to our own size.

What is true knowledge? What is the place of religious language? What is it to live in a technically brilliant age, yet at the same time to be seemingly incapable of inculcating basic moral principles as the building blocks of society? What forgotten insights lie lost and hidden within the Christian tradition that could help us address these questions?

The 'apophatic' way

Here, I believe, we need to reclaim a vital yet frequently-overlooked strand in the great tradition of faith as it has unfolded across the centuries. I refer to the contribution of *apophatic* theology (literally 'the way of denial, of negation') particularly, but by no means exclusively, found in the Eastern Orthodox tradition.

Apophatic theology seeks to say what God is not, in the sense that God transcends any attributes we may ascribe to him—a denial that our concepts match up to the reality of God. This is in contrast to *cataphatic* theology (literally, 'the way of affirmation') which asserts qualities which belong to God's nature and activity—that God is good, life-giving, almighty and so on.[2] The way of negation, it must be emphasised, is in no way to be confused with a way of believing which despises creation or banishes the joy of living. Indeed the true apophatic approach seeks to open us to an encounter in which the hidden God confounds our easy definitions and expectations (the word *apophasis* means literally 'the leap' towards the mystery).[3]

We need to listen to the witnesses who speak to us from those icons of another world—which is in fact *this* world in its true essence. Is there a way of believing that was once alive and vibrant yet has now fallen into oblivion; a way of believing which reminds us that faith, in time, becomes an *unknowing* before it can become a knowing of God; a way of believing that honestly embraces the seeming absurdity of our human life in a broken world? Reflecting on the paradox that in the human search for God we seem to start from a place of unknowing, Andrew Louth makes clear:

> ... this is not in the sense of—as if we started off with little knowledge and found that it increased—but in a more fundamental sense—starting off with an awareness that the One we seek to know is beyond any capacity we might have for knowing.[4]

Entering a new world

To cross the threshold of a church door is increasingly an alien experience for many people. For some, historical curiosity may do the trick. For others a cultural event—maybe a flower festival, a book fair or a concert—will feel safe enough. And, of course, weddings, baptisms and funerals inevitably include many in the congregation who would not usually be there. Certainly 'the regulars' (if we may so refer to the community of Sunday worshippers) will do all they can to make visitors feel welcome, comfortable and at home. And quite rightly so. Indeed in these days of tighter budgets, amalgamation of parishes and often aging congregations—together with the secular and consumer mentality which we live and breathe—the pressure is on to utilise our parish churches for an ever-wider variety and assortment of events, activities and community occasions.

But I find myself registering a note of hesitation and misgiving. It is, I think, to do with not allowing a place of worship to raise questions for the newcomers about the meaning of life. Further, it distracts the regulars from being challenged by their own over-familiarity with matters religious and avoidance of the deeper human issues that seek to be illuminated through religious faith.

Sacred space

Enter many an English cathedral today and soon as likely you find yourself standing at a kiosk, required to pay an entrance fee. Should you be eccentric enough to indicate your intention to say your prayers, it is just possible that the charge might be waived. But there is more. Decked out in a bright sash, an enthusiastic 'welcomer' plies you with leaflets and information as to where you may spend even more money to see the Cathedral treasures, and indeed how to locate the quirkier historical features of the building. By this time you are feeling so thoroughly at home, that it is unlikely that you will have remembered your initial reaction on entering this sacred space.

There is a telling story of a Japanese tourist being shown around a village church by an over-effusive guide:

> I remember sitting at the back of a tiny, isolated church some years ago, on top of a hill in Spain. A Japanese tourist was driven up to the front door and led round the building by a guide he must have hired in the town some distance away. The guide told him, in English, the dates of various parts of the building and then proceeded to dilate upon the superb stone vaulting. The tourist did not even raise his head to look at this. He stared aghast—as well he might—at a horrific, life-sized painted carving of a bleeding man nailed to two pieces of wood. When the guide had stopped talking, the man gestured wordlessly towards the statue. The guide nodded, smiled, and told him in which century it was carved.[5]

I believe the greatest sin for us is to domesticate the things of God, to curb the imagination with simplistic explanations. 'Common sense is the death of religion. It robs faith of its energy and leaves the rest of the world unchallenged.'[6] I look back to a number of occasions in my formative years when I was crossing the threshold of a religious house of prayer, I found myself plunged into another world. That is how it seemed, at any rate, and that was its drawing power. All I wanted was to slip in unnoticed, not to be welcomed, or made to feel at home, and certainly not plied with refreshments.

As a sixth-former at boarding school in Oxford, in place of compulsory chapel[7] which was the norm, we were encouraged one Sunday a term to attend a local church, a number of which were proposed for our choosing. I opted for something exotic. It was a hot and balmy day at the height of summer, Trinity Sunday as I recall. The bells of Oxford were chiming mellifluously, the streets comparatively deserted, and I entered the church at the last minute, finding a seat in the back pew. I was quite unprepared for what followed. Colour, lights, movement, clouds of incense, three clergy wearing birettas—all the ingredients, in fact, of an old-fashioned High Mass.

The Vicar delivered a sermon lamenting the infelicities of the *New English Bible* which had been published only weeks previously. Strange to my mind, none of the congregation took communion, save for a few souls who received from the tabernacle in the Lady Chapel before the Mass began! There was plenty I did not understand, but that seemed not to matter.

Later reflection was, however, to affirm two very powerful reactions which impressed me as fundamental and which I have encountered many places elsewhere. There was above all a real sense that here something was happening. And secondly, there was no doubt that the people present were actively participating in the worship, even if to an outsider it might appear that most of the action was being carried out by those robed at the altar and by the musicians.

The beyond in our midst

If I were to describe the memory of that Trinity Sunday, it was as if entering another world. There have been other times. For instance, discovering Westminster Cathedral at twilight on a damp November afternoon, hidden away behind the old Victoria Street, in the days before the present Piazza existed, with office-workers slipping in for the early evening Mass before taking the underground home. Again, I experienced a sense of utter transcendence at the time of midday prayers when visiting the Blue Mosque in Istanbul in 1965. The same thing happened in Prague in 1967, where an unassuming entrance to what purported to be some mundane civic offices, revealed itself inside to be a Catholic Church, filled to the rafters for a weekday Mass. Not to mention Bethlehem in 1995 celebrating the Armenian Christmas, entrance to which had more security than the departure gates at Heathrow. On all these occasions the same principles have been evident—that here something was happening in which people were actively participating.

There is no doubt that truly to encounter the Christian faith is to enter a world with different dimensions. In recent times there has been some rather puerile talk, often promoted by self-styled radicals, that the Church lives in 'a little world of its own'. Yes, there is always the temptation for navel-gazing and introspection, but this is balanced by the contrary temptation to embrace the spirit of the age in order to court popularity and pretend a phony relevance. 'We now blithely speak of marketing the gospel like any other commodity, oblivious to the fact that such rhetoric betrays a vast intrusion of worldliness into the church.'[8] How quickly such antics fade into the annals of history!

Alexander Schmemann sums it up with characteristic pithiness:

> Whether we 'spiritualise' our life or 'secularise' our religion, whether we invite men to a spiritual banquet or simply join them at the secular one, the real life of the world, for which we are told God gave his only begotten Son, remains hopelessly beyond our religious grasp.[9]

If there is any sense that encountering the Christian faith is to enter a new world, then it must be a world which gives us a new and vastly more abundant perspective upon the world which we already inhabit. Too much religious language, not only in the past, tends to patronise and diminish, rather than to enlarge the human heart.

> This revolt against religious language is understandable; it has suffered as much as any from windy rhetoric in the past. But a lively religious language has in fact always been little to do with rhetoric or even argument; it has been an artistic language—religion has been written in poems, parables, stories—and the decay of religion is inevitably connected with the decay of these.[10]

In the post-modern society we inhabit today we begin to trip up against an ancient archetypal truth which contradicts the popular privatised religious experience that many seem to prefer as they pursue their 'personal journey'. We have described encountering the Christian faith rather as entering a new world, and in entering this new world we inevitably encounter a particular tradition. Peter Mullen puts it well:

> Much of the contemporary world's objection to traditional Christianity is based on the idea the faith must be understood, analysed and accepted before it is practised. This seems to me to be a mistake. It is not a question of deciding anything beforehand from an 'objective' position; as in the case of appreciating the great art of our civilization, it is a matter of entering a world, appropriating certain experiences and learning by heart. This is how any language is learned and it is how we learn the language of the spirit, the language of God. We enter the Church's year, that sequence of festivals and fasts, and we submit to its rhythms.[11]

Sacred Geometry

When we enter a church, we stand in sacred space. In a way we see the contours of our souls enlarged before our eyes. We cross a threshold from the darkness of this world with all its contradictions, to a new place where the light of Christ pervades the limiting darkness, as Owen Chadwick reminds us in his paraphrase of John Keble:

> Let [a church] be fair and ordered that in coming in we have a sense of our own disorder. Let it be dark in comparison of the outward air, that coming in we have a sense of the God who hides himself. Let all be provided for humble kneeling, that coming in we cannot but learn something of lowly prayer; let the chancel be so ordered that coming in, we are reminded of forgiveness through Christ.[12]

But there is indeed a subtlety operating here. Our God is a God who is in hiding; the light of Christ is not necessarily 'in your face' as we might put it today. In the Christian way of seeing things, the allure of instant illumination can easily blind us to the truth of events, in the same way that darkness may conceal unimaginable brightness. At a later point, we shall consider how desiring to know God may, first of all, involve us in a process of *unknowing*. By that token, the perception of the light of Christ pervading the limiting darkness as we cross the threshold of a church may not be handed to us on a plate!

There has been a tendency, nonetheless, to regard church buildings with some suspicion. John Keble notes how remarkable it is that so much of God's Word is taken up with the history of sacred places; not of persons, but of places.[13] After all, it is the people, not the building, who are the Church. Yet this is something of an incongruity, because it tends to disregard the fact that people need homes. The number of property renovation programmes occupying our television channels is a pointer to the way in which buildings serve to express our vision. There is something tangible about a building which is representative of the life that inhabits it. Cardinal Herbert Vaughan, who oversaw the building of Westminster Cathedral at the turn of the nineteenth century, captured the spirit of this when he said: 'Churches are buildings, not merely *in* which, but *with* which, we worship God.'

Worship is unlikely to happen without preparation. And one of the ways this preparation can be effective is an awareness of that which greets us as we enter a place of worship. We are reminded again of what John Keble said of regarding a church building 'Let it be fair and ordered that coming in we have a sense of our own disorder.' Were that always the case! Too many buildings can tell conflicting stories—of not really knowing what the building is for, of confronting the visitor with a sense of tangible chaos, of clutter, of not being a parable of another world, but a rather grim version of this one.

Hunger for beauty

Brother Aidan, once an Orthodox hermit and now an icon-writer living in Shropshire, said in an interview,

> People are hungry for beauty. Part of the vocation of the Church is to be a place of revelation of true beauty. Worship is not just an intellectual grasping of truths but a process of falling in love. ... Beauty is that which opens our eyes to the majesty of God and moves us to desire him.[14]

Today, I seem to hear it being said that our neglect of the importance of beauty is one of the major reasons why fewer people are interested in the Church. One writer says: 'We must stop building beige churches.'[15] Yes, of course, it is a danger that we make an idol of a church building. But perhaps a greater danger is that we make an idol of our own opinions and self-importance.

Idolatry can take many subtle forms: the pictures we make in our minds of God, or the religious phrases with which people can be harangued, for instance. So, in truth, it depends very much on what you think is going on. Consider an icon. Very often in the face of the holy person depicted, be it Christ himself, or the Blessed Virgin or one of the saints, it is the eyes which draw you. What you find is that they are not pointing dramatically up to heaven, nor so full of human emotion as to get in the way. The best icons look straight at you; you find yourself not contemplating, but being contemplated *by them*, by steady eyes which plumb the depths of your soul.

Margaret Visser in her absorbing book, *The Geometry of Love*, while exploring the meaning of consecrated space in the church of St Agnes Outside the City Walls in Rome, touches on this engagement with anyone who crosses the threshold of a church: 'A church is there to remind you, to teach you to pay attention, and to awaken the poetry in your soul. It gives you an exercise in responding'. But that is not to say there is no heart nor centre to what is being disclosed:

> A church is bigger than I am, but it also represents me. Its plan is the plan of a human soul—and often, indeed, the plan of a human body: head, arms, torso. Churches orient us. The word 'orientation'

> means literally 'turned towards the east' (*oriens* in Latin means 'rising,' and so where the sun rises). It is a word derived from church-building: many churches attend to the symbolism of the sun and its movement across the sky, having been built to conform with that cosmic pattern. But 'orientation' has now come to mean any direction. A church knows where its centre lies, and what direction it faces; having direction is always part of its meaning. The French word *sens,* which signifies both 'meaning' (sense) and 'direction', captures the conflation of the two ideas. The direction-ful and meaningful church is an invitation to travel, to stretch our souls and embrace the movement that time imposes upon our lives. Churches express time—but in terms of space.[16]

Sacred space, such as we might encounter in a church, introduces us to a new world; it opens us up to untold mysteries.

II

EXPERIENCING OUR OWN EXISTENCE

> He who does not have attention in himself and does not guard his mind, cannot become pure in heart and so cannot see God.
> *St Symeon the New Theologian*[1]

THE novel *A Whispered Name* by William Brodrick tells the story of an Irish soldier facing a court martial for desertion during the slaughter at Passchendaele in the First World War. On the military panel hearing the trial was a young captain, Herbert Moore, who faced an unenviable responsibility.[2] Now an aged monk in a religious community, ghosts from the past come to confront him, and he finds himself returning to the place where the terrible events of 1917 had unfolded:

> Over the years Herbert grew in understanding. Of himself; and why he had come to Les Ramiers and why he would stay. His first painful lesson was the discovery that for much of his life he'd lived outside himself, reacting to the multiplicity of events, be they mundane or harrying. In the silence of the monastery or working in the fields, he gradually noticed—with a new kind of terror—that within himself he was quite hollow, and probably always had been. Without a jab from the outside, he was nothing. He had no depth … none at least that he was aware of. Reluctantly, fearfully, Herbert began the journey inward, the voyage that cannot be put into words or explained but only lived. And he made another discovery: a richness of existence, intrinsic to his identity and true for all humanity, whose depth was beyond the reach of any calamity.[3]

To live outside ourselves might also be termed missing the experience of our own existence. Rather than an explicit religious experience, it is this, according to Jacob Needleman, which brings the desire for an authentic tradition of contemplation:

> It is not the experience of God that is drawing Christians to contemplative practices, but the experience of existing as such: my

own existence. The discovery is being made that our lives, even at their best, even at their most 'virtuous', do not bring us the experience of our own existence. And the concomitant discovery is being made that in a hitherto unknown place—within the sphere of my own stable attention to myself—I find that I can exist.[4]

These several authors, I believe, are feeling for what we may only describe as the true centre of our existence. What they are also acknowledging is that primarily this is not the place in which we are living, and it is only out of recognising this experience of non-existence that we begin to enter into a new place within ourselves.

As already observed, we move away from the expectation that to enter a church is to embark upon some archaeological exploration when we allow ourselves to register our own reactions to that which presents itself to us. And it is at this point that we find ourselves engaging with our own souls. A vital question for most of us is to ask 'from where do we live our lives?' or to put it another way 'from where do we live in ourselves?'

Aidan Hart in his interview with John Owen redirects us to that inner attention highlighted at the head of this section by Symeon the New Theologian:

> I notice how wonderfully made people are, made in God's image. I feel great compassion, because people are like hungry sheep who want grass, but are living on iron bolts. ... I've been thinking recently that how much we love God depends on where we live in ourselves. If I live in the body, then I am like an animal, and if I live in the brain, then I will get power through my intellect. But if I live in the heart, the heart is paradise.[5]

I suggest this is a question that is rarely asked. We just live; we exist. Things happen and we respond. But there is more. It concerns the habitual way in which we tend to handle all that greets us. In truth, for many people, and for all of us some of the time, we live from the past. Well-used strategies that have helped us to engage with life in the past serve us adequately for new situations—though such engagement may contain a fair proportion of avoidance for the less comfortable predicaments in which we find ourselves.

Naturally, much of this is innate common sense. We learn from our mistakes, and past experience is a good guide to understanding what works for us in many walks of life. However, buried within all this is a state of spiritual disorder which leads us to inhabit a self-contained world. This may manifest itself in terms of inordinate self-protection, self-expression, and self-assertion in relation to others around us. Much of it stems from the conditioning of this world as it has impacted upon us in our formative years. Equally there seems a built-in inability to resist such conditioning, no matter how much we might wish to do so.

Alternatively, there are those who have a tendency to live life from the future. This stems from their imagination no doubt; but it might just happen! This does not necessarily represent the Christian virtue of hope. More often it is likely to be wishful thinking. To enter into a new world, such as we have proposed is represented by sacred space, is to be given the opportunity to experience our own existence afresh, and to consider where it is we are living from.

We are helped in this search when we realise two things. First, the concept of sacred space embodied in the physical and material reality of a holy place is precisely a projection of human nature created in the image of God. Second, this quest for inner attentiveness is in reality a 'letting go' in order to be open to the one who comes to find us. There is the amazing equivalence voiced by Cranmer 'that we may dwell in him, and he in us.'[6]

This offers an entirely new perspective on the reality of the Church, not as some secular institution, but as a living communion which is the very essence of *being*. Moreover, it is this to which the physical reality of a church building or holy place seeks to direct our attention.

> The Church is first of all a kind of space cleared by God through Jesus in which people may become what God made them to be (God's sons and daughters), and that what we have to do about the Church is not first to organise it as a society but to inhabit it as a climate or landscape. It is a place where we can see properly—God, God's creation, ourselves. It is a place or dimension in the

universe that is in some way growing towards being the universe itself restored in relation to God. It is a place we are invited to enter, the place occupied by Christ, who is himself the climate and atmosphere of a renewed universe.[7]

III

A LAND OF UNLIKENESS

How shall we sing the Lord's song in a strange land?
Psalm 137:4

TO be labelled as religious is a dubious accolade, these days at any rate. It may suggest an unnaturally pious disposition or it could conceal an appetite for ecclesiastical goings-on. Inevitably, to many ears, the mention of religion corresponds with unhealthy or dangerous fanaticism in our present world order. Religion, too, speaks of systems and institutions which, given half a chance, mould people in an unearthly approach to life—maybe harmless, but doubtless less than wholesome.

Delving beneath the surface may reveal some of the fault-lines which have fostered such perceptions. How easy it is for faith communities with declining membership to 'spiritually mug' the unaware; anything to keep the show on the road. And the danger with all strategies that seek merely to shore up religious institutions is that opportunities to respond to life's mysteries, as they present themselves, are all too frequently passed by. Again, too many people are patronised in the attempt to present the faith in an accessible way, leaving the deeper rhythms of the human heart untouched.

For the truths of religion to take hold, there is a desperate need for a change of gear. A new spaciousness must be claimed. But this is what the churches seem not to have in the present climate, with the race for financial and cultural survival taking precedence at all times. The Book of Genesis recounts the story of Jacob, the son of Isaac, who connives to cheat his elder brother Esau out of not only his birthright, which would include inheritance rights, but also his father's covenant blessing—all by cunning and deceit. Esau falls for it; it is a prime example of short-term gain at the cost of losing something seemingly less tangible, but of immeasurable worth in comparison with a bowl of lentil stew! How can we also throw away our birthright for a mess of potage?[1]

Too easily religion can be employed as a distraction from life, rather than a true engagement with it. Jean-Pierre de Caussade in his classic treatise on the spiritual life speaks of 'the sacrament of the present moment':

> The present moment is always the ambassador who declares the order of God. … Everything is a means and an instrument of holiness; everything without exception. The 'one thing necessary' is always to be found by the soul in the present moment.[2]

This says something about the starting point for a new engagement with the life of the spirit. It is echoed by St Augustine, writing in the fifth century:

> Men go abroad to wonder at the height of mountains, at the huge waves of the sea, at the long courses of rivers, at the vast compass of the oceans, at the circular motion of the stars and they pass by themselves without wondering.[3]

A new disposition

Am I right to suppose that, for many people, religion is seen as something imposed, a hierarchy telling you what to do and how to behave? It is a perception that needs radical reshaping, for the primary business of religion is to inculcate in the heart of the disciple the disposition to receive, to embrace that which is not of our own envisioning; that, indeed, which lies outside the world-view which we presently entertain.

This disposition to receive can be applied to a number of dimensions to which the Christian tradition relates and in which it flourishes: the world we inhabit, the human phenomenon, the aspirations of the human heart, the stories we tell to extract meaning from existence, and the presence, or otherwise, of God.

What we find so hard is to locate a starting point from which this whole way of being in the world can unfold. How easily we confine ourselves within certain intellectual premises which actually overstep their expertise. In his book *Why us?* James Le Fanu explores the power and limits of science to penetrate the deep mysteries of human existence, and he concludes his study with this telling observation:

> The vibrant optimism of that Enlightenment view of man has evaporated. Indeed, we could almost be said to live in an age of 'counter' enlightenment—where the prevailing scientific view maintains that man's sense of himself as an autonomous independent being is no more than an illusion generated by his brain, and the joys and agonies of human love no more than a device for the propagation of his genes.
>
> Many factors have contributed to that cultural pessimism, but the most obvious feature that distinguishes modern man from Voltaire and his contemporaries is the ascendancy of scientific materialism, and the loss of there being a non-material reality that transcends our everyday concerns. We have lost that sense of living in an enchanted world.[4]

Overlaying the Christian template upon this observation reinforces the point, throwing a clearer light upon what we are feeling for: Aelred Squire reminds us that 'one of the primary purposes of Holy Scripture, considered as a vital whole, is to show man to himself.'[5] Similarly, Laurence Hemming opens a book about Christian liturgy with the arresting sentence: 'To pray is to ask to be made ready to hear.'[6] Each of these instances tempts us to believe that there is a new dimension to existence to be received.

The nature of faith

History reminds us on many an occasion that the moment the penny drops is unexpected, and frequently shattering at the same time. St Paul on the road to Damascus is thrown from his horse by a dazzling light which challenges him over his persecution of the followers of Jesus. St Francis, in the ruined church of St Damiano, finally recognises the significance of the inner voice that had been unsettling him ever since his futile attempts to find glory as a knight on the battlefield. The result of these experiences is a new vision and purpose that becomes all-consuming, and is transformed into faith that drives their lives with a single-mindedness they had never known. I am moved by a definition of faith from Werner Pelz in an address at Cambridge University in 1964:

> Faith—in the Old, and I believe in the New Testament—is the passionate directedness of the whole of one's being towards one's vision, one's hope, one's desire. It is that fusion in which we become whole and wholly reach out beyond ourselves towards the not-yet-realised, towards the not-yet; seeing what is not yet as more real than everything that is.[7]

This does, however, leave a number of objections unanswered which was evident at the time from the questions that followed this address. What is to be said, for instance, of the passionate directedness of Hitler, or other ruthless dictators? By what means can a choice be made between such conflicting 'visions'? Replying to this Pelz underscored the terrible reality that the mad vision of Hitler occurred in the very heart of Christian Europe where Christian faith and dogma had been taught and argued over for centuries. Confronted by a destructive vision, the fall-back position is to begin moralising (which he equated with a highly sophisticated form of moaning!). In the end the only realistic challenge to such an evil vision is to be confronted by a life-giving and more persuasive and burning vision.

That continues, I believe, to be the case fifty years later. In the present day, in a world increasingly dominated by materialism and religious fundamentalism, moralising still seems to have little effect. What vision is there to sustain hope and creative living that eclipses the destructive visions so rampant in the world today?

A land of unlikeness

'How shall we sing the Lord's song in a strange land?' (Ps 137:1) This verse from one of the most evocative of the Psalms touches a deep place in the human heart. This plaintive cry of the exiles of old is one that is being voiced progressively in the brave new world which we inhabit. Religious communities in minority situations have habitually tended to survive either by assimilating the values and aspirations of the surrounding culture, or by adopting a ghetto mentality, inward looking, self-contained, barricaded against the world around. Increasingly, as the generations follow, the original sense of identity is lost.

It is not difficult to draw a parallel with the situation of the churches today. Here in England we face shrinking congregations, fewer resources, and generations that have not known faith. And churches easily fall for the safety of the ghetto, or become indistinguishable from the secular values around.

The weightlessness of God

One of the aspects of society today is a craving for instant satisfaction. If they are going to have any involvement with church, people expect this from religion as well. Often the churches tend to go along with this—anything to keep the show on the road. But the seeming benefits may be very short-lived, and tend by their very nature to detract from any deeply rooted faith.

'Our passion for understanding', writes Pastor Peters, 'has slowly but surely dismantled the mist and mystery to leave God exposed and vulnerable to the simple, the mundane and the domestic'.[8] And it is not hard to draw attention to some habitual ways in which God is domesticated. As I suggested previously, to domesticate God is to cut God down to our own size. To domesticate is to reckon to understand God and God's ways, rather than to 'stand-under' God as one who gently questions our whole manner of being in the world.

David Wells offers a thoughtful contribution to ways in which the evangelical movement in the United States has become heavily invested in the mindset of modernity; he comments: 'The growing weightlessness of God is an affliction that is neither peculiarly Protestant nor peculiarly Catholic but is the common form in which modernity rearranges all belief in God'. He points to the prevalence of 'designer religion' where 'an interest in religion can be nothing more than a fascination with ourselves as religious beings quite distinct from our standing before the true God'.[9]

This is well exemplified in a study of desert and mountain spirituality where the author, Belden C. Lane, admits his frustration with certain images of God so prevalent in our time:

> I am increasingly uncomfortable with current images of God found in books and workshops that mix popular psychology with a theology wholly devoted to self-realisation. They seem to reverse the first question of the catechism I studied as a child, declaring that 'the chief end of God is to glorify men and women, and enjoy them for ever.' I do not really want a God who is solicitous of my every need, fawning for my attention, eager for nothing in the world so much as the fulfilment of my self-potential. One of the scourges of our age is that all our deities are house-broken and eminently companionable. Far from demanding anything, they only ask how they can more meaningfully enhance the lives of those they serve.[10]

In effect, we domesticate God when we behave as if we have God 'all buttoned up', a pawn in our own plans, and so turn God into an idol which legitimises our own pretensions.

Designer religion

Spirituality has become almost an industry in itself. The Churches are sprouting spiritual gurus at a rapid rate, and we are bombarded by new publications which offer the most recently fashionable spiritual techniques and their heroes. Some popular spiritual approaches and self-help techniques amount to highly-individualised mystical 'joyrides' with little grounding in the whole tradition of faith proclaimed in the Creeds.

In reaction, some have even questioned whether it is really legitimate to speak of 'the spiritual life' at all in the context of Christian faith. Alexander Schmemann writes of the goal of Christian life as appropriating the gift of the Holy Spirit in the sacramental life of the Church:

> We say 'Christian life' and not 'spirituality' because the latter term today has become ambiguous and confusing. For many people it means some mysterious and self-contained activity, a secret which can be broken into by the study of some 'spiritual techniques.'[11]

In a similar vein, Heather Ward, in the chapter 'Narcissus at prayer', confronts an over reliance upon a personal faith story which drives a wedge between experience and doctrine.[12] Douglas Dales, in a recent book exploring the spiritual theology of Bishop Michael Ramsey, comments that Ramsey also was 'cautious about the burgeoning interest in "spirituality" that was becoming fashionable in the closing years of his life.'[13]

Living in a strange land

How then, do we 'sing the Lord's song' in this strange, post-modern, land? Living in a strange land, a land of unlikeness, is well captured by St Bernard of Clairvaux:

> See, we are before him as though we were not, as nothing and emptiness. In this land of unlikeness what business are we engaged upon, Lord God? I see the human race from sunrise to sundown circulating in the traffic of this world; some seek wealth, some run after privilege, others are captivated by the gratifications of popular favour.[14]

We could be tempted to believe that all this is part of what we have to take on board in order to be open to a new future. On the contrary, it is certainly not to suggest that we simply abandon what we might describe as a 'God-forsaken world' for a fantasy comfort zone. Moreover, there is a level on which we have to embrace this sense of displacement; we must look into our own hearts. For it is our hearts which contain an inner defilement and disease that contribute to our restlessness in a seemingly hostile world (cf. Mark 7:14–21).

IV

THE UNKNOWING OF FAITH

> God cannot be grasped by the mind.
> If he could be grasped, he would not be God.
>
> *Evagrius of Pontus*[1]

IT IS a sad affair that in our world of technological precision and instant sound-bites we have lost sight of a far richer approach to the nature of reality, to the confrontation with truth, and to the rhythmic register of language.

Which tells us more? A scientific text-book or the imagery of a poem; a dictionary definition of the word 'adoration' or a love-song; to watch a concert or a football-match on television, or to be present in the arena or the stadium? The answer, of course, is that each has their place, and it depends upon what you are dealing with. But for many people there is probably no contest!

Religious language

This is the mindset we are invited to adopt in our approach to the truth of the existence of God. Here, too, it depends with whom you believe you are dealing. Is God just one more object, however wondrous or powerful, within the breadth of human experience, a mere being amidst other beings? Or is there that in God which is quite beyond all human intelligence? Classical theology has made a firm distinction between God in his essence *(ousia)* which surpasses all knowing and is beyond words, and the activities of God *(energeiai)*, his involvement in human affairs in a tangible way.

All this touches on the difficulty of using religious language in a scientifically orientated world. Yet this is not to suggest we should give up talking about God. it is more about the way we do it. Can God-talk engage the human imagination in a way that opens us up to that which lies beyond our horizon, without needing to have everything buttoned up and under control? Karen Armstrong has written: 'Religious people are always talking about God and it is important that they do so. But they also need to know when to fall silent.'[2]

Here we have to observe how religious language is working for us. Does it make sense to speak of language describing the indescribable? Certainly there is constant reference in the Christian tradition where language operates in this way. We find an example in an ancient hymn from Vespers on Christmas Day:

> How shall I tell of this great mystery?
> He who is without flesh becomes incarnate:
> The Word puts on a body;
> The Invisible is seen;
> He whom no hand can touch is handled;
> And he who has no beginning now begins to be.[3]

This in itself is evidence of the way language works in worship, in a register quite different from everyday discourse. A useful reminder, also, that the prevalent fashion for wanting to use the language of the street in church, all modern and relevant, does not always work, because the language of worship actually functions in a different way. In fact this is a prime example of language being instantly accessible and 'marvellously forgettable'[4] Does it really work to move our souls to a new place?

Here is signalled the need for a proper reticence in the way we speak of eternal things. We even find this within the teaching of Jesus in his preference for the parable and the riddle to giving a straight answer to those who questioned him. As with the question 'Does God exist?' it is easy to get trapped by the question in such a way that whatever answer is given cannot convince. Denys the Areopagite is helpful when bringing us to an awareness of the limitations of language.[5]

Via Negativa

Essentially Denys says we know God by not knowing God. And before we plunge in too deeply, it is worth remembering how our ordinary human relations function. Here too, there is knowing and unknowing. The closer we are to another person, the more we feel we have got to know her or him. And it is very easy at this point to feel we have the other person buttoned up. It is natural then to get possessive, and to suppose we understand her or his every whim. But there are usually surprises along the way. For some this is too much to bear and a threat to their inner security. It can be at this point that a relationship flounders and gets into difficulty. But it can also be a growing point, with the realisation that there is some 'unknowing' with which to be engaged. *This* expression of *via negativa* which we term 'unknowing' can prove equally liberating in our standing before God. It is a way of being before God without limiting God's essence to any particular definition. Here is the gateway to the gift of the prayer of contemplation.

Via negativa[6] attracts considerable misunderstanding and suspicion. Is it little more than disguised atheism? Does it serve to obscure the direct and robust proclamation of God's Word? Is it a distraction from the clear mission of the Church in our post-modern world?

Here we rather seek to point to *via negativa* as a vital strand in a healthy theology and as a milestone on a path of spiritual growth which takes the material world seriously, but not necessarily on its own terms. Whilst I believe that the 'great tradition' of Christian spirituality embraces the *via negativa* as a complementary strand to more affirmative and dogmatic expressions of the faith, we may also highlight it as a way of safeguarding against tendencies to domesticate God into little more than the projection of our own hopes and ambitions, and so preparing us for the long haul on our Christian pilgrimage.

The Eastern tradition

The flavour of *via negativa* may be illustrated with a number of contributions from the wealth of evidence within the traditions of the Eastern and Western Churches as a whole. Whilst the term itself appears in the writings of Meister Eckhart (1260–1329), it is within the apophatic theology of the Eastern tradition that the 'negative way' most fully influences the impact of its entire spiritual tradition. It is here that we begin.

The image of Moses as he ascends Mount Sinai in cloud and deepening darkness is a fundamental image.[7] Bishop Hilarion Alfeyev cites the early exponents of the apophatic tradition, Gregory of Nyssa and Dionysius the Areopagite (or Denys or Pseudo Dionysius), who speak about the divine darkness 'as a symbol of God's incomprehensibility.'[8] Only Moses, after separating himself from all things and ascending the mountain, could enter the darkness and encounter God who is outside everything, 'who is there where there is nothing.'

'Cataphatic (affirmative) theology', on the other hand, is that which speaks of the attributes of God—eternal, good, life-giving, almighty—whereas 'apophatic theology' proceeds by saying what God is not, in the sense that God transcends any attributes we may ascribe to God. Here Alfeyev writes:

> In our understanding of God we often rely upon cataphatic notions, since these are easier and more accessible to the mind, but cataphatic knowledge has its limits. The way of negation corresponds to the spiritual ascent into the depths of God, where words fall silent, where reason fades, where all human knowledge and comprehension cease, *where God is*. It is not by speculative knowledge but in the depths of prayerful silence that the soul can encounter God, who is 'beyond everything and who reveals himself to her as *in*-comprehensible, *in*-accessible, *in*-visible, yet at the same time as living and close to her—as God the person.

Vladimir Lossky has likewise described how negative theology or the apophatic way

> is not merely a theory of ecstasy. It is an expression of that fundamental attitude which transforms the whole of theology into a contemplation of the mysteries of revelation. It is not a branch of theology ... it forbids us to follow natural ways of thought and to form concepts that would usurp the place of spiritual realities.[9]

The Western tradition

Turning to Western spiritual traditions, Meister Eckhart was influenced by Celtic traditions in Germany and some of the twelfth-century women mystics. He taught a four-fold way, of which the second path was 'Via Negativa: Letting Go and Letting Be'. He had much to say about the need for detachment: 'There, where clinging ends is where God begins to be'.

Clearly he is not talking about indifference, or an unhealthy dislike of the material world, nor a letting go because things are bad, but precisely because we want to *cling* to them and possess them for ourselves, rather than allow them to reveal to us what lies beyond. Eckhart would have no place for *via negativa* without it being preceded by his first path, *via positiva,* which is an appreciation of the joy and rapture which is due to God in God's creation. From these two paths then issue *via creativa*: giving birth from within, a mutual generation from our union with God. It is a similar path to the Eastern understanding of *via transformativa,* whereby God works compassion through us to build the new creation.[10]

To underline this, Henri de Lubac quotes St Anselm: 'When we say that God is ineffable, it does not mean that we cannot say anything about him!'[11] Indeed, says de Lubac,

> … nothing is worse than a premature 'negative' theology. … God is not ineffable in the sense of being unintelligible: he is ineffable in the sense of being above everything that can be said of him. … The ineffability of God is only another name for absolute transcendence. Silence comes at the end—not at the beginning.[12]

The way of detachment

At a similar period in England, the *Cloud of Unknowing* is another example of apophatic theology, where the way of negation is the first stage on the path to perfect contemplation. Here the unknown author quotes Dionysius: 'The most divine knowledge is that which is known by not-knowing.'[13]

It is, however, in the Carmelite tradition in the West that we find the more developed unfolding of this way of detachment. Despite the freshness of many a person's initial call to walk the Christian way, sooner or later our human attachments and appetites begin to present a problem. St John of the Cross was a powerful proponent of this idea in *The Ascent of Mount Carmel:*

> Since the things of this world cannot enter the soul, they are not in themselves an encumbrance or harm to it; rather, it is the will and appetite dwelling within that causes the damage when set on these things. (Bk 1, Ch. 3)
>
> To reach union with the wisdom of God a person must advance by unknowing rather than by knowing. (Bk 1, Ch. 4)

Detachment is about learning to love God as God, and not for what God gives us:

> As we shall explain in speaking of the night of faith, a person has only one will and if that is encumbered by anything, the person will not possess the freedom, solitude and purity requisite for divine transformation. (Bk 1, Ch. 11)[14]

Unknowing and astonishment

In the first letter of St Paul to Timothy, we read the following referring to the coming manifestation of Christ in all fullness: 'He who is the blessed and only Potentate, the King of kings and Lord of lords, who alone has immortality and dwells in unapproachable light, whom no man has ever seen or can see' (1 Tim. 6:16). Here, too, it is important to emphasise, as Lossky reminds us, that the apophatic way does not finally lead 'to an absence or to an utter emptiness, for the unknowable God of the Christian is not the weary impersonal God of the philosophers.'[15] Dionysius speaks of his entering on the way to the Holy Trinity 'which is to bring him to a presence and a fullness which are without measure.'[16]

Frequently the apophatic tradition finds expression in the sublime paradoxes of some of the early hymns, 'You alone are unknowable, for you have generated all that is knowable'.[17] In the *Confessions* of Augustine we find, 'What then is my God? ... most hidden ... and most truly present; unchangeable, yet changing all things; ever active, and ever at rest.'[18] Indeed the mystery beyond all mysteries is, 'yet closer to us than we are to ourselves'.[19]

John Donne, too, touches upon that resolution which lies beyond all earthly distinctions:

> And into that gate they shall enter, and in that house they shall dwell, where there shall be no Cloud nor Sun, no darkness nor dazzling, but one equal light, no noise nor silence, but one equal music; no fears nor hopes, but one equal possession; no ends nor beginnings, but one equal eternity.[20]

V

PARTING WELL MADE

Man's last and highest parting occurs when, for God's sake, he takes leave of God. *Meister Eckhart*[1]

GOING into the desert places is likely to involve some process of letting go of our image of God—or maybe just finding that God is absent. Said the twelfth-century mystic Meister Eckhart, 'Man's last and highest parting occurs when, for God's sake, he takes leave of God.' Taking leave of God. It is not actually a new experience to encounter the absence of God. The Psalms echo this time and time again:

Up, Lord, why sleepest thou;
awake, and be not absent from us for ever.
Wherefore hidest thou thy face;
and forgettest our misery and trouble.
Psalm 44:23–24

Indeed, so too in the poetry of R. S. Thomas. But here God is not so much hiding as just not experienced, for the poet speaks of God as 'That great absence in our lives.'[2]

The dark night of faith

In his Spiritual Canticle, St John of the Cross testifies to this darkness as the experience of many on the Christian way. But in the dark night of the desert eventually there comes a tranquillity, that inner calmness and sense of release to which Carlo Carretto testifies in his *Letters From the Desert.*[3] And in the Spiritual Canticle the night brings the whistling of love-stirring breezes:

My Beloved, the mountains,
and lonely wooded valleys,
strange islands,
and resounding rivers,
the whistling of love-stirring breezes,

the tranquil night
at the time of the rising dawn,
silent music,
sounding solitude,
the supper that refreshes, and deepens love.[4]

In the wilderness, we have the space to trust that our inner vision will be cleansed and refined. Faith takes on a new dimension. In place of faith being regarded as a series of propositions about God that we have to believe, we begin to see something of the true nature of this virtue. As Werner Pelz remarks, faith is 'seeing what is *not-yet* as more real than everything that is.'[5] To return to the story of Jesus in the wilderness, resisting the temptations of the devil, this 'not-yet' God is the one to whom Jesus is faithful. He refuses to take stones—those idols and false images—and turn them into bread, as if they were the real thing.

As proposed in Chapter two, one of the reasons we happen not to know God very well is that we do not know ourselves very well; we do not realise our need for Divine Love. Yes, we are happy enough to talk about a kindly, benevolent God and we pout a bit when he does not seem to treat us as we think he should. And that is good enough reason that sometimes we need to take leave of God and our false images of God. The truth is that some of the ideas and pictures that we have of God prevent God revealing Divine Love to us. We look for God in the wrong places. How can there be an exchange of love between a God who is not able to be God for us, and we who are not ourselves before the holy one?

Palladius, a historian of early Egyptian monasticism, tells this story, a paraphrase of which is included here:

> There was once a mad scullery maid who worked in a convent. She becomes the frequent recipient of scorn and abuse from the whole community of sisters. She eats only the scourings and scraps which are left over, never even chewing her food, and drinking only dishwater. She is dressed in rags and sleeps on the kitchen floor. She is, in a word, disgusting. But there comes a day when strangely

> under God's guidance, a certain saintly brother called Piteroum recognises her as a holy person and actually the spiritual centre of the convent, and suddenly she vanishes into the desert and is never heard of again. Though regarded by one and all as an idiot, her self-effacement makes actual idiots of all her sisters in the convent, for they have failed to see her true worth. She becomes as nothing. It is only then, in her final absence, that the community recognises that she has been, in fact, the true and necessary heart of the convent who has made the community possible—the sponge and empty desert who has absorbed its dross and excess. Her very 'being' is perceived 'to be nothing', and she is the quiet, unrecognised wisdom who is perceived only as a negation.[6]

Make of it what you will. But maybe when the God we thought we knew leaves the scene, we then start to realise whom it is we are missing, and the taint of Original Sin is set aside. 'We are pilgrims in search of our own hearts.'[7]

VI
LIVING WITH ABSURDITY

> God's place is in the 'kingdom of the impossible', in the 'kingdom of absurdity', somewhere where a totally different logic applies than in 'this world'—the logic of the paradox... The dead come to life, the blind see, and those who say 'we see' have become blind.
>
> *Tomáŝ Halík*[1]

LIVING with absurdity is something thrust upon us. Much of it belongs to the way life is—its untidiness, its lack of resolution, its messiness. A fair portion of the business that crowds our days we could happily stop doing tomorrow, and the mundane is where our lives take place. The encounter with faith often originates in the most mundane of circumstances—a chance encounter, an off-the-cuff remark. Why is it that one person responds to the call of faith, and another thinks the believer is from a different planet?

Much is heard these days about the Church needing to be more relevant, but this is a somewhat slippery notion; no matter how much the clergy try to be one of the boys, or one of the girls, this innate absurdity of their position will Never change. And if it does, the Church will have become so sanitised that the words of T. S. Eliot ring all too true when he spoke of 'having the experience, but missing the meaning.'[2]

The pathos of the cross

For some believers the absolute absurdity of life is simply solved by the Resurrection of Christ. Here is the 'take it or leave it' answer. God raised Jesus from the dead, so the absurdity and pathos of the cross is wiped out. I do not think that will do—where is the mystery?

Indeed, one of the troubling elements about some of our revised liturgies and modernised orders of service is that they are so loaded with tabulated good news that they do not reach into the awkward nooks and crannies of absurdity in our hearts. The new Order for Daily Prayer: 'Strengthen us in our stumbling weakness' may cover some of our shortcomings and genuine honest confusion.[3] But it is not the full story for all of us all of the time. What about the devices and desires of the heart?

Living with the sower

Recall the well-known Parable of the Sower recorded in all three of the Synoptic gospels.[4] Some of the thrill of this parable is its uncompromising sense of abandon. Here is the sower scattering the seed, on the most unpromising ground, a rather absurd enterprise. It is a dreadfully hit and miss business; but the hits actually score above the misses, and in the end yield a bumper harvest.

Werner Pelz[5] believed it more than likely that Yeshua[6] or Joshua (as Pelz preferred to identify the prophet of Nazareth) saw himself in the image of the primeval sower scattering the seed. He spun and wove tales about the absurdities of human life in order to gather a rich harvest and to capture his listeners with the promise of a kingdom, which they might seek above all else. It is an image of Jesus as the artist, a supreme artist, a spinner of tales, a teller of stories which continue to weave a new web around our lives, and give a fresh perspective as to who we are, and how we might perceive the world. The beauty and gracefulness of his words reshape our deformed world as an act of artistic creation.

He paints for us a different world where we may sit as loosely to things as do the birds of the air, and the flowers of the field; a world which is as hard to enter as it is for a camel to pass through the eye of a needle. Yet it is a world into which those who have not earned a place, or paid their way, or done a full days' work are the very ones who find themselves summoned to the banquet, because everyone else has something better to do. It is an upside-down world where the wastrel son is welcomed home, where a merchant risks all for the pearl of great price; a world where the very moment we find ourselves at the mercy of events or threatened by an assumed enemy, the person I question turns out to be our neighbour.

In the end, the words of Joshua / Jesus in the parables unfold the promise of forgiveness. For they lure us beyond the limited boundaries within which we have been content to live, into a hope and vision of a future beyond our narrow satisfactions. We are like a man who is forgiven his debt, and offered a second chance. We are like the blind given back their sight, or have the withered hand healed, or the paralytic who takes up his bed. They are all parables of forgiveness, in that the world is given back to a person. Not so they may pick up their old ways of doing things, but to start again on the venture of faith.[7]

By faith alone

Consider Abraham, who sets out in his old age—he knows not where—on the journey of a lifetime. To live by faith is to discover the meaning in the going forward. The one Great Tradition of the Church is a living thing. And we should not get too fussed when others remain confused by it all, yet somehow put a foot on board. I like the comment of Vincent Donovan in the introduction to *Christianity Rediscovered—an Epistle from the Masai*, and really a parable for the mission of the Church in a secularised world: 'In working with young people in America, do not try to call them back to where they were, and do not try to call them to where you are, as beautiful as that place might seem to you. You must have the courage to go with them to a place that neither you nor they have ever been before.'[8]

Today it is so hard for the words of the one we call Jesus to touch people with their beguiling promise. The name of 'Jesus' has been blunted by over-familiarity. And yet there's still enough religious folk memory around waiting to be tapped, but all too often we are happy to settle for what is less than satisfying. Moreover there are signs today of a more militant, though disguised, atheism, where the secular fads and trends of the day quietly displace the ultimate values which are rooted in God alone. How can the human imagination be engaged once again in this changing world? For it is by keeping alive our imagination that we are sheltered from the cold draughts of debilitating doubt and despair, giving us the energy to reach out to the future.

Mr Golightly's Holiday, a recent novel by Salley Vickers, succeeds in doing just that. I quote, without I hope giving too much away, if you have not read it:

> Looking outside [Mr. Golightly] saw a spider's web, one of many whose delicate dentations decked the cottage windows. The spider spun its web simply to trap flies—but what was designed by nature for a natural function may take on more than nature's ends. The fragile structure had caught, in its subtle mesh, the drops of rain from a morning shower and the diamond beads shone in the sun, fragments of some larger, profounder, more luminous light. ... And had not his own son, his own dearest creation, been such a spinner of spells, a weaver of stories to catch human hearts?[9]

It pays to spend a little time to remember with gratitude some of those whose vision of faith has excited you—has engaged your imagination and sparked your vision—has goaded you on to persevere through the dark nights and days of seeming absurdity that assail us all. And what is it about Joshua, the spinner of tales, the weaver of new patterns that still captivates you?

The path of paradox

Cyprian Smith has portrayed the paradox of Jesus as our own paradox: 'Once we stop seeing Jesus as a mystery, we also stop seeing ourselves as a mystery; and that means we have lost hold of the truth.'[10] Returning to *True Resurrection* by Harry Williams CR, a sentence caught my eye in the Preface. Williams, as we would expect, describes his approach of grounding his theology in experience and self-discovery, and comments that in writing it he was interested to discover his approach had been closer to the tradition of Eastern Orthodoxy than to that of Western Christianity. He explains that it had long seemed to him that Western Christianity, for all its talk of analogy or paradox, had felt too much at ease in its assumption that its dogmatic formulations were representationally adequate descriptions of mystery. He adds, 'I have found too among the Eastern Fathers an emphasis on *unknowing* [my italics] as the inevitable medium of our knowledge of God.'[11]

In 1972, when the book was first published, I imagine these words did not have the slightest impact on me. But looking back now, I see them as a kind of theme of what slowly began to emerge as a new dimension to Christian belief and practice. Almost exactly that same year, I remember listening to Paul Scofield reading extracts from *'Letters From the Desert'* on the radio. His mellifluous tones seemed to give added significance to the printed word.[12] Indirectly it was my real introduction to the desert tradition and the Little Brothers of Charles de Foucauld. De Foucauld himself (1858–1916) was formerly a French cavalry officer, who was later drawn back to the desert in the early years of the nineteenth century serving as a priest in Morocco and Algeria, eventually living a solitary life among the Tuareg tribes people, welcoming all, 'good, bad, friend or enemy, Muslim or Christian.'

The good soil

If we may return to the Parable of the Sower, it has become a truism to remind ourselves today that we are in the business of sowing seeds, and not necessarily being too impatient for the harvesting. But something which always strikes me about this parable is not the moralistic interpretations as to who is the bad soil and who is the good soil. It is the fact that it is *the good soil* in which the seed actually takes root. And good soil does not happen by chance. Only by tilling the soil adequately, as enthusiastic gardeners will remind us, only by preparing the ground will the seeds take root. Anyone who has been to the Holy Land knows that; there are rocks everywhere and cultivation of the terraced fields is a hard and painstaking business. Hence a further reason for the parable. It is perhaps significant that as his ministry unfolded, Jesus moves on from the spinning of tales for the multitudes, and spends increasing time with the few, the little group of disciples, tilling the impacted soil of their stubborn hearts.

Alan Ecclestone has talked about the importance of 'that life prior to prayer.'[13] How easy it is to assault the populace with religious words, quite unearthed from their situation. How easily we theologise about Christ in conceptual form before he is allowed to touch and expose the genuine contradictions in our hearts. Are people given room and space to reflect upon the real things they may be bringing with them into their praying and wrestling with God? There is a need to affirm what we might describe as the 'Old Testament' of people's lives.[14] Here is our story writ large. We have to share again the faith of Abraham and the prophets; we have to acknowledge the reality of our disobedience to the truth, and our hankering after false gods; we find we are re-living the experience of bitter exile, even experiencing the utter absence of God. Far too often the figure of the Christ is plucked from thin air, almost as a religious label, a token, who offers easy salvation.

We have to recapture this sense of a people who are watching and waiting for the one as yet unknown in the manner of his coming; the one who is to come into the present situation of our own lives and communities. But then we panic and resort to quick-fix salvation to fill the pews.

There is a great work to be done in our generation in preparing the ground. And of this Charles de Foucauld remains a powerful icon. He once wrote: 'Direct evangelisation is impossible at the moment; the only life possible is that of Nazareth ... by his presence Jesus will sanctify, silently this vast country.'[15] Charles saw his vocation as a missionary task, but one with a difference: he was not there for the sake of any crude conversions. Indeed the irony of his life was that during his desert ministry he converted no one and attracted not a single follower, despite dreams of starting a community—and was almost crushed by the outcome. He was a silent and unheard man of words, who in his lifetime was 'nothing'. He died in isolation, as had another Man of Sorrows, murdered by brigands in 1916 amidst the people he had greatly respected and served. Today his hidden presence lives on among the Little Brothers and

Sisters of Jesus[16] in some of the poorest as well as some of the most secularised cities of the world.

Preparing the soil is an essential ingredient in preparing for new growth. Here we connect with the 'Old Testament' dimension of people's lives. Here we find ourselves sharing the journey of faith with Abraham and the prophets. The story of Abraham and Isaac is indeed memorable.[17] Following his promise to Abraham in his old age, that he is to be the father of a great nation, whereby his descendants will be more numerous than the stars, God sets out to test Abraham's ultimate loyalty by leading him to sacrifice his only son and heir, Isaac, by whom the promise could be fulfilled. The story is surely the ultimate in pathos, though Herbert McCabe reckons it all ends rather lamely with God saying it was an almighty con just to see if Abraham would pass the test![18] The neat ending of the ram caught conveniently in the thicket to be the sacrificial offering takes away the mystery, the glimpse into the darkness of God. Though McCabe cites the powerful ending to Wilfred Owen's poem about the 1914–18 war ('Parable of the Old Men and the Young'), in which Abraham gets so fascinated with the ritual sacrifice of war in the name of God that he will not listen to God's word at the eleventh hour to lay down the knife: 'But the old man would not so, but slew his son, / And half the seed of Europe, one by one.'

The ultimate paradox

Nonetheless we are left with the question that faced Abraham: how could Isaac, being sacrificed and killed, bring forth his promised descendants? How could Jesus, murdered on the cross continue his mission of love? Can we step outside the demands of love in order to commend love's beauty? This surely is living in the unknowing of faith, and walking the path of paradox.

Here is the concluding paragraph of Herbert McCabe's sermon to which I have just referred:

> To believe in the resurrection is not to hold the view that God is so clever that he can even bring a dead man back to life. It is to believe

> that, whatever we mean by God, his ways are dark and mysterious, that he leads us, sends us life and meaning, through death and absurdity. To recognise this truth about the human condition, to see it and be obedient to it, as were Abraham, the servant in Isaiah, and Jesus, is to begin to understand what God is all about.[19]

It would be too simple to say that because Christ is risen, we can short-cut all that; because we live post-resurrection we can forget the struggles of the heart represented by the Old Testament. Almost by sleight of hand, resurrection faith is replaced by triumphalism; we have got all the answers. On the contrary, all we have is the living answer of a Risen Christ, an answer which is as true for those who believe as it is hidden for those who cannot.[20] But that does not stop us living in quiet faith that God is in control according to God's ways.

VII

THE IMAGINATION OF OUR HEARTS

> I am convinced that the broadest possible exercise of imagination is the thing most conducive to human health, individual and global.
>
> *Marilynne Robinson*[1]

RELIGIOUS language speaks of being human in a quite remarkable way: we are 'frail children of dust' yet made in the image of God; sinners yet saved; mortal yet destined to put on immortality.[2] In other words, it is a part of our human condition that we are compelled to talk about love, hate, hope, fear, wonder and amazement. We also need to reflect on failure, guilt, and forgiveness. We need to make reference both to our hearts and our souls. All this is just as true as the language of science—but it kindles our imagination in an entirely different way. Maybe this is too simplistic. In the same way that religious language can become mean, trivial and patronising, so too scientific language, which at its best is exploring the grandeur and wondrous complexity of the natural world, can shortchange its audience. Religious language is both a way of knowing and unknowing the reality of God; the language of affirmation is tempered by the *apophatic* tradition which qualifies every assertion about God by saying 'yet this is not it'.

Marilynne Robinson perceives the same tension revealed in the scientific mind-set. In her essay 'Imagination and Community' she is pondering the value of the many books that litter her shelves, both read and unread. Recently she had bought a book titled: *On What Cannot Be Said: Apophatic discourses in Philosophy, Religion, Literature and the Arts*.[3] She makes the wry comment, 'The title itself is worth far more than the price of the book.'[4] But the point of her essay is that amidst her bookshelves and stacks of magazines that she can never bring herself to throw away:

Mrs. Norman E. Sims
15206 Clondesley Court
Silver Spring, Maryland 20906

> … there are any number of articles suggesting that science, too, explores the apophatic—the reality that eludes words—dark matter, dark energy, the unexpressed dimensions proposed by string theory, the imponderable strangeness described by quantum theory. These magazines might be titled 'Learned Ignorance', or 'The Cloud of Unknowing' or they might at least stand beside Plato's and Plotinus's demonstrations of the failures of language, which are, paradoxically demonstrations of the extraordinary power of language to evoke a reality beyond its grasp, to evoke a sense of what cannot be said.[5]

This surely encourages us to recognise a common approach and sensitivity across this 'language barrier' when we reach out to describe the indescribable.

The language of faith

But why all the religious talk? Surely we can talk about these things just as *human* values? That is certainly true, but the passion that lies at the heart of religious tradition expresses the belief that here is the best and truest way to talk about these human values. The language of faith unwraps the business of being human in the form of stories and myths handed down. It is a fact that many of the pictures we have of God actually get in the way of God making his love known to us. This is another way of saying the language we use about God has to grow up, and be allowed to speak for itself in its own register, to rediscover its own authentic voice, rather than aping the rapidly expanding language of science and technology. The stories and parables that Jesus told are, for the most part, a direct road into our imaginations. Equally, how often do we find Jesus saying: 'It was said to you of old … but I say to you *this* … love your enemy, turn the other cheek.' He engages us in a process of spinning and weaving, reshaping reality so that we see it differently. We can see how this overlaps with the attempt of Werner Pelz to describe the imagination:

> And I do believe that this is precisely the supreme function of the imagination … to twist that which is not yet reality, to twist and spin it, to spin tales, to weave patterns in order that men's imagination may be kept alive, and sheltered from the cold draughts of

> doubt and despair. For me imagination is that fusion of passion and intellect, when the emotions have become intelligent, and where intelligence is passionate.[6]

All in the imagination

Here we must sound a cautionary note. Is not an over-emphasis on the place of the imagination simply another term for glorified wishful thinking? 'In your dreams!' runs the current colloquialism. And indeed, there is a distinction to be drawn between different uses and understandings of the human imagination.

There is no disputing that according to the biblical writings, we are frequently led astray by the imaginings of our hearts. Excessive self-assertion, self-expression and self-protection are all indications of a spiritual disorder to which we are enslaved. This fall from grace is described in the early chapters of the Book of Genesis. It is a fact of life that 'the inclination of the human heart is evil from youth' (Gen. 8:21). Likewise in the New Testament, the Magnificat, the canticle sung at Evensong in the Book of Common Prayer, brooks no illusions: 'He hath scattered the proud in the imagination of their hearts' (Luke 1:51). Despite the best will in the world, the chances are that we will misuse the good gifts with which we are endowed—even our imaginations, as we have already noted in the eloquent phrasing of the prayer of confession at Morning and Evening Prayer: 'We have followed too much the devices and desires of our own hearts.' But in no way does this remotely suggest that the human imagination is other than our bridge to a new vision of the world. It is waiting to be received as a sacrament of God's invigorating presence.

A sacrament, according to the BCP Catechism, is 'an outward and visible sign of an inward and spiritual grace given unto us as a means whereby we receive the same, and a pledge to assure us thereof.' Or, as we might say, a sign, with a promise attached. The worship of the Church is all about a re-kindling of the great tradition of prayer and worship which has been handed down through the ages; essentially it is an expression of the corporate imagination of God's people. In the sacraments the story of our redemption is told and told again:

> The worship of the Church satisfies this very real need for support for our Christian convictions by providing the imagination with an experience that presents the truths of faith in a powerful and convincing way. It is a great foolishness to ignore the imagination, because the world, the flesh, and the devil go after us through our imagination.[7]

By the same token, Austin Farrer suggests that when Christians gather to hear the word preached, it is the rich fabric of images that they rehearse and apply. When they baptise and when they celebrate the Holy Supper, they are engaging with God by enacting images:

> The Eucharist, more than any other Christian practice, gathers up all the images and expresses the whole story of creation and redemption in a way that incorporates the participants into the story and so begins to move them into a life shaped by the image.[8]

Farrer goes so far as to say that the Supper 'is not a special part of our religion, it is just our religion, sacramentally enacted.'[9]

To ask if this story is true, in the end is not to go searching for historical evidence or proof, but to observe what happens to us as we are caught up in this story. Do we find here a fuller truth about what it is to be human in *this* world, fuller than any scientific textbook can offer? It is a story that, in faith, we have to let wash over us again and again, until it invades our imagination and becomes a very part of who we are.

Two-way traffic

Truth, according to the Christian tradition, is mostly apprehended on two levels. There is the big picture, and we need regularly to be refreshed by having our eyes and hearts lifted to a vision of wholeness and holiness. How easily we become so swamped by the minutiae of each day that we lose an overall sense of direction and purpose. And yet the devil is in the detail; the real work of living out the Christian way behoves us to attend to the little things that can make all the difference in the way we relate to those around us.

These two levels may be represented for us by the public liturgy (offering of worship) of the Church, and by the personal response of meditation, pondering and prayer that we carry out in the chamber of our hearts (cf. Matt. 6:6f). We need both. Indeed the two feed off each other and there is a glorious confusion of heaven and earth, if we may put it this way, in which the liturgy of the Church and the liturgy of the heart are holding us.

In the liturgy, the everlasting worship that takes place in heaven is made available to us on earth, and yet through participation in the worship of the church our hearts are lifted up to heaven. 'When things of heaven are wed to those of earth', announces the *Exsultet* in the Easter Vigil.[10] There has always been a vital tension between earth and heaven. Certain expressions of faith, though, are bent on abandoning this naughty world, this vale of tears, and waiting to be transported to some distant heaven. Others, so-to-speak, are so earthbound that the clouds entirely obscure the stars.

> Vast, mysterious, and mostly unknown as the universe is, we are neither aliens nor strangers in it. It is our alienation from God that makes us see the world as if we were aliens. It is our estrangement from him which leaves us with this haunting sense that we are alone, strangers in a cold and indifferent universe.[11]

There is a tale in the book of Genesis relating how the people build an enormous tower in an attempt to reach up to the heavens and make themselves known to God, lest they be scattered over the face of the earth. We read how God has to come *down* to have a look at it, saying almost 'Well, there's a thing; what confusion!' (Gen. 11:1–9).

An interesting and parallel observation can be found here when Metropolitan Anthony Bloom highlights the tension and contrast between Gothic and Romanesque church architecture. His interviewer was speaking about the experience in the Gothic cathedrals of Western Europe of being drawn upward within a vast cosmic scale filled with light, finding here an example of sacred art that guides humanity towards knowledge of the real. The stained glass, the upward movement of the columns, the cross-vaulted forces of the ceiling all transmit a sense of greatness and mystery. Metropolitan Anthony responded:

> I have always been revolted by Gothic … and for a long time I did not understand why. But when I was living in Paris I came to understand it. All that aspiring, aspiring upward—yet not all the way. The Romanesque church is an utterly different idea. In Romanesque something has already come down to man: love.[12]

The point here is that in the older Byzantine basilicas there was a centralised space beneath a descending dome, with a fresco of Christ the All-powerful, which was intended to bring heaven down to the society of men. A feature which was reinterpreted in many Romanesque churches where the presence of Christ and the apostles is depicted, reflecting the manner of a feudal court, but clearly involved with the existing world order. An example of a Romanesque church, reflecting the Byzantine influence with a series of five domes, may be found in the French cathedral of St-Front at Périgeaux.[13]

Earth and heaven

This two-way traffic between earth and heaven is an unfolding theme in Genesis 28:10–17. In Jacob's dream, when he spent the night near Haran with a stone from the earth as his pillow, there was a ladder set up on the earth and the top of it reached to heaven:

> and behold, the angels of God were ascending and descending on it! And behold, the Lord stood above it and said 'I am the Lord, the God of Abraham your father and the God of Isaac. The land on which you lie I will give to you and to your offspring … and in you and your offspring shall all the families of the earth be blessed.'

And when Jacob awakes from his sleep, he says:

> 'Surely the Lord is in this place, and I did not know it.' And he was afraid and said, 'How awesome is this place! This is none other than the house of God, and this is the gate of heaven.'

We find this image introduced again at the beginning of St John's gospel when Jesus is calling his first disciples, and we are given a preview of who this new prophet might be. Nathaniel expresses surprise that Jesus seems already to know him, but is told 'You will see greater things than these. Truly, truly, I say to you, you will see heaven opened, and the angels of God ascending and descending on the Son of Man' (John 1:43–51).

Throughout these pages, we have found ourselves returning to the paradox of the unknowing of faith: 'O world unknowable, we know thee' writes Francis Thompson (1859–1907) in his poem *In No Strange Land*. This heavenly world is beyond our reach, and yet descends into our midst. In our desire to know God, we must begin as if not knowing him 'but as standing before a mystery that is, and will remain beyond our understanding.'[14] When we approach the presence of God with this disposition, then we are open to receive that which we have not conjectured for ourselves, but which comes down to meet us. This is a dimension quite different from 'the quest of the self' which inhabits the spiritual yearning of so many in this generation, whether religious or secular in its manifestation.

The True Self

Out of the crumbling world of the philosophy of the Enlightenment, there has grown this new fascination for the quest of the self, as the gateway to all things eternal:

> In this new spiritual quest, it is the self which is the conduit into the spiritual world. It is through the self that seekers imagine themselves to be peering into, and experiencing, the eternal and by doing so hoping to find some meaning. It is supposed that in the self we receive intuitions about the eternal.[15]

What, then, is the alternative to this quest of the self? David Wells is quite clear:

> The alternative connection to what is ultimate is, of course, revelation. In this view, it is not the human being reaching up to seize the meaning of life, but God reaching down to explain life's meaning.

> In this understanding, there can be no speaking of God, no speaking of meaning, before his speaking to us is heard.[16]

This notion of God reaching down, in contrast to the human aspiring to heaven, is the revelation of the divine love, as Metropolitan Anthony insisted. This is further clarified by the existence of two different words in Greek for the nature of love. The first is *eros* where the self is at the centre, seeking, longing for that which will satisfy. Whereas the Greek word *agape* is the selfless love of God incarnated in Christ and reaching down to us through the work of the Holy Spirit. True meaning, then is given in *agape,* never seized through *eros.* And here we find grounded the reality of Christian hope:

> Hope has to do, biblically speaking, with the knowledge that the the age to come is already penetrating 'this age,' that the sin, death and meaninglessness of the one is being transformed by the righteousness, life and meaning of the other, that what has scarred and blackened it, is being displaced by what is rejuvenating and transforming it.[17]

It is through the worship of the Church that this vision, this big picture, is renewed and made concrete in the celebration of the Liturgy week by week, and through the subsequent meditation and prayer of the faithful where these truths are taken to heart.

VIII

ACTUAL PARTICIPATION

> The Kingdom of heaven is peace and joy in the Holy Spirit ... Acquire inward peace, and thousands around you will find their salvation.
>
> *St Seraphim of Sarov*[1]

THERE IS a popular perception in the minds of some who occasionally attend church, and indeed some clergy, that worship is essentially an activity that is laid on in order to encourage people to think of God. It would surely follow, therefore, that the more worship is lively and relaxed, user-friendly and easily understood, the more attractive for those who may be tempted to come. What is required, so it is believed, is for the experience of worship to be managed to ensure everyone feels at home all the time. Rather too often these days announcements and explanations, instructions and light-hearted asides liberally punctuate the liturgy so that nobody appears to be left in any doubt as to exactly what is going on. Imagine going to the theatre and having such interruptions littering the play you had gone to watch! That which is supposed to encourage participation in the liturgy actually inhibits true engagement. Congregations become onlookers, not participants.

Manufactured spontaneity

There are a number of issues here. The first touches on the nature of spontaneity. Many clergy and worship leaders are frankly suspicious of set forms of worship. Depending on churchmanship and background, some believe that spontaneity can be induced by changing the odd words here and there just to keep people on their toes, and to suggest the minister is not staidly bound by the texts provided; a practice which usually turns out to be irritating and distracting as it tends to interrupt the instinctive responses that the faithful may be pursuing in their hearts.

Others prefer to abandon liturgical orders entirely and make it up as they go along. Better, they say, to be led by the Spirit and speak as you are moved at the moment. Such an approach is surely more sincere and authentic. It is remarkable, though, how undistinguished the Spirit's manner of communication often turns out to be; and moreover how frequently repetitive. And this from those who tend to frown upon 'set forms' as disregarding the stricture to avoid 'vain repetition like the heathen do'![2]

Lurking behind this approach is a perception that the style of worship in the early church has been lost as the churches have become more established over the centuries. Was it not all more free and easy, spontaneous and informal in those halcyon days? The first Christians had not been saddled with all these wretched 'set forms'; they just made it up, in the power of the Spirit, as they went along.

In his book, *Worship as a Revelation*, Laurence Hemming seriously questions this view:

> The early Christians considered themselves to be the true successors not so much of the worship of the synagogue, but the Temple. In this this they believed themselves to be reflecting a tradition they had received directly from Jesus and what he communicated, often in secret, to the Apostles. Historically the liturgy of the Western Church (as indeed in the East) abounds with references to, and indications of, this belief.
>
> The common conception of the early Church as in many ways ad hoc, as groups of Christian men and women coming together informally to sing hymns, pray, break bread and bless wine, is quite false.[3]

His point is that persecution and the sacred character of what took place, often behind closed doors, meant that little was committed to writing at the time. But more fundamentally, he reveals that the real roots of Christian worship lay in the worship in Solomon's Temple in Jerusalem—in other words, it was anything but ad hoc.

This touches on a fundamental ingredient of worship. The earlier reference to the view that worship is something we lay on to lead us to God has a number of implications. Is an act of worship predominantly the occasion for exploring how we can use religion as a resource for improving our common life? Indeed does not this mirror the mind-set of a generation which reckons to be able to manufacture all it needs for the good life? Hemming sees this as having infiltrated the way we approach even our sacred worship, whereby it 'can be got hold of and improved, or altered, to produce *better* or *more effective* outcomes'[4]

Worship in the new creation

We are being led to a new perspective. To worship is not 'us laying on an experience'. No, it is to participate in something which is already happening.

> Worship happens in heaven and is available to move us to worship in union with the angels and the saints. Worship is not just something aesthetic that we organise to make us think of heaven.[5]

True worship, I believe, is an evangelistic activity in itself. I often encouraged the congregations for which I had responsibility to stop panicking as to how to 'get more people in', and to trust and believe a little more in what they were actually doing. To be confronted, as a visitor, with a worshipping community who seem to know what they are about and are getting on with it, even if it leaves you somewhat at a loss to know exactly what is going on, is surely a profoundly more revealing encounter than having everything explained before it happens and interspersed with constant stage directions. Worship of this calibre has a drawing power of its own. The questions come afterwards.

Moreover, as Hemming points out, to know *about* the God disclosed through the liturgy is not the same as knowing God *in* the liturgy:

> The liturgy discloses an understanding of God as he reveals himself to be, in Christ, in a knowledge that can only be gained through faith, not deducted or derived by reason or a rational act of self-positing.[6]

Such an understanding underlines how the contemporary way of knowing about people and things contrasts strongly with the

Christian tradition in which knowledge comes as the fruit of participation or communion.[7]

In a review of Hemming's book, Dr Alcuin Read suggests that we are no longer liturgical; we no longer understand what it is to belong to a people who acts: 'Today we seek to comprehend and explain and decide what we do in our churches but it is utterly questionable whether our people experience the liturgical revelation of Almighty God'.[8] As Hemming puts it 'the liturgy is nothing less than the ordinary and continual revealing of God's truth.' And if this is so, then it cannot be a mere vehicle for our own self-expression, or 'enjoyed' as a form of Christian activism. It is rather the ground and foundation of all living theology.

What is it to participate in the Liturgy? One approach is to introduce a multitude of varying congregational responses, on a seasonal or thematic basis, often in a didactic context. But does this actually serve to lift the common prayer of the community? It can tend to become a parrot-style response to the worship leader. Another approach is to ensure that as many individuals as possible are doing things in the course of the liturgy without much rhyme or reason. But it is easy to forget that actual participation is a thing of the heart, not simply jobs for the boys and girls.

Especially, those sitting in the pews participate in a vital way in the liturgy by keeping the prayer going, just as much as acolytes, readers and musicians. Says Hemming, '*Actuosa participatio* means fully to participate in what the rite itself participates "in" and makes us present "to"'.[9]

The church needs to have confidence in its own distinctive character and tradition. The consumer culture in which we are set functions by encouraging people to pick and choose what is for their own good. There is a tendency to go for the window-dressing and miss the guts in issues of faith. This attitude has its liberating side, but we have to question whether basic moral and human values are subject to such random selection. Snippets of Fauré's Requiem lace TV consumer advertising, which has the effect of inflating the product, and reducing yet one more lifeboat to the divine mercy and grace to near absurdity. It would be unhelpful if Christian worship tried to prove its relevance by offering a 'religious atmosphere' in which to pursue our secular agenda.

'Auxiliary' worship

This leads us to reassess the nature of worship. I am compelled by this understanding of worship not as something we 'lay on' to make us think of God, but as something that is already happening when life is caught up in the mystery of God. If this is so it may be claimed that the one area where we might expect the Church to display confidence in its own distinctive character most fully is in the offering of worship.

Yet William Barlow, an Orthodox Christian, during his search for faith encountered what he describes as a generally low expectation of worship, albeit that people still found reasons for going to church: 'This meant that they were condemned to believing in spite of their worship.' Merely seeking to make worship more relevant did not seem to him to be getting us anywhere. The fundamental flaw, Barlow believes, is that worship has come to 'take on an auxiliary role.' People are often heard to say that they go to church to 'recharge their batteries'. Worship becomes an activity for 'buttressing belief' or 'an appeal to Man's aesthetic sense, rather than to his instinct and capacity for worship.' Worship that emphasises chiefly the externals of ritual, and worship which essentially appeals to the emotions to reinforce a conversion experience, both 'appeal to the least stable part of Man':

> Consequently, they did little to promote that sobriety which is proper and essential to a steady and constant relationship with God and involvement in the divine realm. With sobriety thus set aside, the way was open for a nostalgic attachment to things which were not at all essential to worship.'[10]

All true Christian worship, and supremely the Eucharistic Liturgy, as testified to in the Book of Revelation is nothing less than a participation in the worship of heaven. As such it requires of us a disposition of openness to what is being revealed. In a word, it is to participate 'in the perfect unity of the heavenly praise, in expectation of the longed-for *Parousia*[11] of the Lord Jesus Christ.'[12]

IX

WORSHIP AS REVELATION

> Although you have not seen him, you love him; and even though you do not see him now, you believe in him and rejoice with an indescribable and glorious joy. 1 Peter 1:8

THERE IS a story of how, a thousand years ago, the Grand Prince Vladimir of Kiev in Russia wanted to find a religion worthy of his people. Accordingly he sent some followers abroad to find the true religion. After visiting one country, they reported: 'There is no joy among them.' Further south in Europe, they complained that here too the worship, though more satisfactory, was without beauty. Finally they journeyed to Constantinople. As they attended the Divine Liturgy in the great Church Hagia Sophia (Church of the Holy Wisdom),[1] they discovered the object of all their searching: 'We knew not whether we were in heaven or on earth, for surely there is no such splendour or beauty anywhere on earth. We cannot describe it to you; only this we know, that God dwells there among humans'.[2]

Those visitors had found themselves present at worship that was transforming. It was as if life itself was revealed to be fashioned according to an entirely new blueprint. They knew as they left that they had been in a place where eternity touched time, and it had happened in their midst.

How this contrasts with some approaches to worship in our own day! As I have already noted, there is a trend abroad that everything must be instantly understandable. How can it be? We proclaim the peace of God *which passes all understanding*! If everything is explained before it happens, then the mystery is destroyed. Indeed the prayers themselves found in some of the newer liturgies take on this didactic character: everything is increasingly wordy, and more and more like an education lesson.

Earlier in my ministry as a priest, I believed the right way to draw adults to the faith was to explore the big questions of life: is there a God? Why evil? Why suffering? Where are we going? Now, I am not so sure. Even if a cogent answer is provided to all these questions, does it actually help? Christianity is not a string of watertight answers to the knotty problems of life. The heart of the Christian faith lies in the mystery of the Church, and the mystery of the Church is revealed in the worship of God the Holy Trinity. True worship has a transforming power: 'we knew not whether we were in heaven or earth.' It is the sense of participating in something which is being opened up to us and happening in our midst which counts.

The mystery of the Church

The presumption throughout these pages is that the life of the Church in all its fullness is a visible sacrament of a hidden world, which in truth is this world of flesh and blood that we inhabit, seen in the context of eternity. But what is the nature of this mystery of which we speak?

All too often, the mysteries of faith, like all other mysteries, are assumed to be capable of a rational outcome, in the manner of a murder mystery or a crime story. In Graham Greene's affectionate novel *Monsignor Quixote* the deposed communist mayor, Sancho, is bending the ear of his priest companion, as they picnic in the late afternoon sun: 'What puzzles me, friend, is how you can believe in so many incompatible ideas. For example, the Trinity. It is worse than higher mathematics. Can you explain the Trinity to me?'[3]

How many attempts at explaining the image of the Holy Trinity have you and I encountered in untold sermons? The clover leaf, or trefoil, with its three 'leaf-lets', for example. Three in one, and one in three. But we know that this really does not tell us anything. Fr George Rutler once put it: 'God cannot be diagrammed.'[4]

Consider a human being. How do we understand a human being? Well, a human being can be X-rayed and it may tell us quite a lot. But it will not explain who this person is. On the other hand a portrait may reveal much more, because a portrait reveals something of what it is to be related to others. It is the personality that expresses itself. So too, God is not a formula; the task of apprehending the divine love is beyond all diagramming. Peter Mullen said, 'Doctrines are not only formulae: they are like pictures or music. We return to them again and again for they are truly inexhaustible. And every time we attend to these mysteries we are changed by them.'[5]

The mystery of the Holy Trinity

Yet what happens when we talk about the mystery of the Holy Trinity? Look at the Athanasian Creed: 'And in this Trinity none is afore, or after other: none is greater, or less than another; But the whole three persons are co-eternal together: and co-equal.'[6] Yet the Trinity is not a puzzle we have to solve. One of the early Christian monks, Evagrius, said this: 'God cannot be grasped by the mind. If he could be grasped, he would not be God.'[7]

No, the doctrine of the Holy Trinity celebrates the divine life which is beyond our understanding; and yet by the grace of Christ and the enabling of the Spirit is now made present to us. It is much more like a new world which we are called to enter.

A lingering fragrance

The Narnia books by C. S. Lewis are illuminating in this regard. In *The Lion, the Witch and the Wardrobe* the children hiding in a wardrobe from a grumpy housekeeper suddenly feel very cold. When they look they see there is no back to the wardrobe and they climb through to this new land of Narnia in Winter. Here the White Witch rules with menace, but Aslan the Lion is on the move, breathing new life.[8] This is the type of mystery that the Trinity is about, and we are more likely to find meaning in the vigour of such stories than in vast tomes of theology.

But Lewis also once told his god-daughter Lucy that Narnia is not a strict allegory, where everyone and everything is meant neatly to represent something else. That would turn them into a puzzle with a solution. Then he said something very important. His stories were meant to be more like 'a flower whose smell reminds you of something you can't quite place.'[9] Now that is more the sort of affinity we should associate with the mystery of the Holy Trinity. It is almost as if much of the time we are not living in the place where we truly belong, and yet we know that our everyday world has a solidity which we cannot abandon.

In St John's Gospel, Jesus says to Nicodemus: 'Indeed, God did not send the Son into the world to condemn the world, but in order that the world might be saved through him' (John 3:17). Because God comes into the world, he saves us. He saves us from being anything less than God wants us to be. He saves us from the illusion that only what we see immediately before our eyes is real, that we can explain God on our own terms. God cannot be so diagrammed.

To practice the catholic faith, is not merely to believe things *about* the Holy Trinity. Much more, it is to find ourselves drawn to *participate in* the life of the Holy Trinity. The mystery of the Trinity is love, pure and undiluted. Here we find the very truth of our existence and are drawn to share in the divine glory as did the seekers for the true religion in Hagia Sophia.

Glory beyond description

Every Sunday is a mini Easter Day, the day of the Lord's Resurrection. This day, so Christians believe, marks the crossroads of history. Yet the magnificence and wonder of what occurred lies beyond the normal categories under which we classify events. So much so that Lesslie Newbigin once declared: 'Indeed, the simple truth is that the resurrection cannot be accommodated in any way of understanding the world except one of which it is the starting point.'[10]

Not knowing what actually happened on the morning of the Resurrection is a state of affairs with which the modern world cannot cope. We read the witnesses who spoke of the later appearances. But what of the moment itself? In the tomb. Behind the stone that sealed the grave. What happened?

Because we cannot know, many react by saying that *something* must have happened—some event in this world like all other events. Such responses are by now familiar. Maybe grave robbers stole the body? Maybe Jesus had been comatose, not dead? Or maybe the Essenes, a monastic-like community near the Dead Sea, had sent two men in white to remove the body by stealth to bury it again secretly in the Judean desert. This would, after all, be a stimulus for others to proclaim a resurrection. Or maybe the tomb, occupied or empty, was irrelevant; what happened was in the minds of the apostles: the memory and impact of Jesus' teaching and his final sufferings, had so impressed them as to overcome any sense of loss on their part. All of these theories have had their proponents. And all of them seek to explain the mystery in terms of the unfolding of events as we usually perceive them.

Silent witness

It is notable that in classical art there are very few paintings which tackle the actual moment of the Resurrection. For the very good reason that it is impossible to imagine. Those that do are heavily bathed in symbolism. Think of Piero della Francesca's famous painting of Christ emerging from the tomb, a banner in his right hand, his posture displaying a silent and utter stillness, all of which is taking place with no human witnesses. The only other figures in the painting are the four soldiers guarding the tomb, fast asleep.[11] The scene suggests a world that has grown tired, and weary, and is blind to what is truly happening, the breaking-in of a new world order, that of the Risen Saviour. We may call to mind the Easter Collect: 'Almighty God, who through thine only-begotten Son Jesus Christ overcame death, and opened unto us the gate of everlasting life ...'[12]

The convincing ingredient that colours the Gospel accounts of the first Easter, and the days that follow, is their untidiness in the attempt to convey that which cannot be contained in words, and yet compelling us also to believe. The early witnesses, on the whole, first come to believe because of what they do *not* see. And when they do come close to this living truth, at first they do not recognise Him: Mary Magdalene in the garden, the disciples on the road to Emmaus, Thomas in the Upper Room doubting to the last moment.

It is significant that we find exactly the same range of reactions to the birth of Jesus, as we do here to his resurrection: shepherds and wise men saw, and knelt in wonder. Others were entirely indifferent; and others, like Herod, were hardened in their hearts, and tried to destroy. So, too, at Easter, the risen Lord was seen by some, but not by others. Some believed and it changed their lives, others were puzzled; and others were either indifferent or hostile in the extreme. And so it has ever been.

The hidden secret

What then, may we ask, is the hidden secret revealed in the Resurrection? There is a saying of Hugo of St Victor, a twelfth-century mystic from Saxony: 'Love is the eye!' he said, 'Love is the eye!'. If we look at things through the eyes of love, we see, we understand, we engage with the mystery; but to look at things with eyes that are jaded, or cynical or bitter, we shall not see, nor shall we properly believe nor understand. It is this that we find underpinning the Resurrection stories. It also explains why in the end Thomas did see, and many others at the time did not. Thomas desperately wanted to see, that he might believe; others really did not want to see and to them no sign was given. Capture again those words of St Peter on the nature of our believing: 'Although you have not seen him, you love him; and even though you do not see him now, you believe in him and rejoice with an indescribable and glorious joy' (1 Peter 1:8).

From earliest times Christians have gathered through the night of Easter Eve to recall the story of God's saving work, from creation through to the death and resurrection of our Lord Jesus Christ. However the Easter Liturgy is not merely a presentation of God's work. It is meant to be a real experience of new life for the worshipper, a passing from darkness to light which offers hope to all the faithful.

The Easter Liturgy opens with the Service of Light, where the kindling of the new fire leads to the lighting of the Paschal Candle. In a darkened church the Candle is carried through the congregation, as one by one individual candles are lit from it, reaching its climax with the chanting of the *Exsultet* or the Easter Proclamation or of Christ's joyous resurrection. The Liturgy then unfolds with Vigil readings, a Baptismal Liturgy which declares our union with Christ in his death and resurrection, and finally the Liturgy of the Eucharist.

Fr John Hunwicke captures the mystery of that 'Night truly blessed, who alone wast worthy to know the time and the hour',[13] marked as it is by the same awed reticence as the accounts of the Gospel writers:

> The most stupendous event in the history of the cosmos—the most terrible wonder in the elapse between the initial and final big bangs—is never actually described. The Lord's Resurrection is, as it were, wrapped in veils. Jesus' burial may be described … but no television camera, no recording historical pen, no purported eyewitness, intrudes into the darkness and mystery of the cave-tomb. … The greater the miracle and the greater the wonder, then the more need for a veil to shield our eyes. … The naked brightness of the divine reality would be too much for us as now we are. But as we kneel at the altar, every Eucharist is Easter and the Lord is the risen and invincible one—and he whispers to each of us, as he whispered to Mary in the garden, the Name he has given us; and for a moment the veils become very thin, and he walks through every locked door into the upper room of each one of us.[14]

This hidden scandal of particularity, in all its manifestations, is something that we shall never shake off or unravel. If we are honest, it is precisely how the most meaningful moments in our own lives and relationships take form and vivacity. It is certainly true in the ways in which we engage with the Christian tradition, and it continues to be the channel by which the churches respond to the divine initiative through worship and the celebration of the sacraments.

EPILOGUE

The Orthodox theologian Alexander Schmemann once drew attention to the fundamental paradox of 'the basic religion that is being preached and accepted as the only means of overcoming secularism is in reality a surrender to secularism.'[1] In other words, the function of religion is being recast in terms which are those of secularism, as *help*, rather than *truth.*

Might things be otherwise in our response to the beyond in our midst? How much has worship come to play merely an auxiliary role in human life? Is there any expectation at all of the possibility of being 'astonished'? Why does the clerical mind-set so often appear as faintly patronising?

The Reverend Julius Lestrade, a character in the novel *Ingenious Pain,* is an eighteenth-century country clergyman. During a period of absence from his parish, he writes to a friend fearing that he discharged his office as a conscious hypocrite:

> A lawyer may perhaps practise his profession without much faith in the law or a soldier attend to his duties without believing his war to be a just one, but the man of the cloth cannot decently continue without his faith. I know, my friend, you are wagging your head and saying if such were the case half of the divines in England would have to relinquish their positions. I sometimes think that what I fear most is that I could live quite contentedly without religion. Is this the spirit of our times? An overweening age?[2]

Now I suspect there are more clergy who pose to themselves Julius Lestrade's question, in one form or another, than might admit it and it has often led me to ask what exactly is going on in this seeming mismatch. But what is striking in the novel is that Julius Lestrade has the space and independence to face such doubts. And maybe what presents itself to us as an irritation at the Church's quaint ways, or frustration at keeping an ecclesiastically smiley face in an uncomprehending world is, in fact, a signal of a more fundamental confrontation with the nature of hope amidst human frailty and mortality.

Here it is that the shoe often pinches in the modern church. Given the more managerial mindset of ecclesiastical institutions, does it not get harder to claim that independence, let alone to use it creatively? For me, at least, this is where 'the way of unknowing' finds its relevance. To be able to say 'I believe' yet 'this is not it' introduces the prospect that one day we may be astonished, and this is to live by hope. Without the *cataphatic* tradition of affirmation, this would be wishful thinking; held in tension with the *apophatic* tradition of negation, faith holds before us the possibility of being drawn to the unapproachable light in sheer astonishment.

It was recorded in a short appreciation of Hugh Maycock, one time Principal of Pusey House, Oxford that 'He saw astonishment as the basis of all religion: when men and women lost the capacity to be surprised and astonished, they could no longer be religious.'[3] That astonishment, it seems to me, is unlikely to be of substance in the contemporary secular world, without our also embracing in some form the *via negativa*, where faith becomes an unknowing before it is a knowing of God.

> The true knowledge and the true vision of what we seek consists precisely in this—on not seeing: for what we seek transcends all knowledge, and is everywhere cut off from us by the darkness of incomprehensibility.
>
> *St Gregory of Nyssa*[4]

NOTES

Chapter I. Gates of Mystery

[1] Andrew Louth, *Introducing Eastern Orthodox Theology* (London: SPCK, 2013), 114.

[2] See Bishop Hilarion Alfeyev, *The Mystery of Faith* (London: DLT, 2002; *R* Oxford: Stephen's Press), 24f; also Timothy Ware *The Orthodox Church* (London: Penguin, 1993), 63.

[3] Olivier Clement, *The Roots of Christian Mysticism* (London: New City, 1993), 38.

[4] Louth, *op. cit.*, 4.

[5] Margaret Visser, *The Geometry of Love: Space, Time, Mystery and Meaning in an Ordinary Church* (New York: Viking, 2001), 1.

[6] Stephen Mitchell, 'Seduced by the Siren of Common Sense' *Sea of Faith* website. http://www.sofn.org.uk/printme/press/siren.html.

[7] Anecdotes abound relating the success of compulsory chapel in turning pupils off religion, though in my experience, this was not the case. For others, however, it may have served to root such young people in a tradition with which they were later able to re-engage and appropriate (or not) for themselves.

[8] David Wells, *God in the Wasteland* (Leicester: IVP, 1994), 58.

[9] Alexander Schmemann, *For the Life of the World* (London: DLT, 1966), 13.

[10] Nicholas Mosley, *Experience and Religion* (London: Dalkey Archive Press, 2006), 19.

[11] Peter Mullen, *The New Babel* (London: SPCK, 1987), 107.

12 Owen Chadwick: 'What cannot be, Love counts it done'. Sermon preached on 25 April 1976 at the centenary of the dedication of Keble College Chapel: *Christian* Vol. 3 No. 4 (1976), 313–6.

[13] John Keble, cited by Chadwick *op. cit.*

[14] James Owen, 'The hermit next door', interview with Brother Aidan Hart, *The Daily Telegraph*, 22 April 2000.

[15] Robert Barron, quoted by Ronald Rolheiser in 'Beauty as God's language' *The Catholic Herald*, 12 September 2004.

[16] Margaret Visser, *op. cit.*, 15.

Chapter II. Experiencing our own Existence

[1] St Simeon the New Theologian, *Writings from the Philokalia: on Prayer of the Heart*, trans E. Kadloubovsky and G. E. H. Palmer (London & Boston: Faber & Faber, 1951), 158.

[2] Deserters were routinely executed by firing squad.

[3] William Brodrick, *A Whispered Name* (London: Abacus, 2009), 304.

[4] Jacob Needleman, *Lost Christianity* (Shaftesbury: Element Books, 1990), 117.

[5] James Owen, 'The hermit next door', interview with Brother Aidan Hart, *The Daily Telegraph*, 22 April 2000.

[6] Book of Common Prayer: Holy Communion, 'Prayer of Humble Access'.

[7] Rowan Williams, 'The Christian Priest Today' in *Glory Descending: Michael Ramsey & His Writings* (Norwich: Canterbury Press, 2005), 164.

Chapter III. A Land of Unlikeness

[1] Gen. 25:29–34. Esau 'sold his birthright for a mess of pottage'. Though this phrase does not appear as such in the *King James Bible*, it first figures as a chapter heading in the *Matthew Bible* of 1537, and is found in common usage, meaning 'to sell yourself short'.

[2] Jean-Pierre de Caussade, *Self-Abandonment to the Divine Providence* (London: Fontana Library of Theology and Philosophy, 1971), 66–70.

[3] Quoted by James Le Fanu in *Why us?* (London: Harper Press, 2009), xiii.

[4] Le Fanu, ibid., 251.

[5] Aelred Squire, *Asking the Fathers* (London: SPCK, 1973), 10.

[6] Laurence Hemming, *Worship as a Revelation* (London: Burns & Oates, 2008), 1.

[7] Werner Pelz, 'A New Reformation—Beyond Theology?' Sermon at Great St Mary's, Cambridge, 15 November 1964, 2. Werner Pelz (1921–2005), a Jewish refugee from Hitler's Germany, lived in England and Australia and was an unlikely priest in the Church of England for 12 years. He completed a doctorate in Sociology in 1974 and was appointed a university lecturer in Australia, but also drew widely on the insights of poets and mystics. His writings (with Lotte Pelz) included *God is No More* (London: Gollancz, 1963) and *True Deceivers* (London: Collins, 1966). He died in 2005.

[8] Pastor Peters, 'Domesticating God by the words we use in worship', *Pastoral Meanderings Blog*, 8 February 2014. http://pastoralmeanderings.blogspot.co.uk.

[9] David Wells, *God in the Wasteland* (London: IVP, 1994), 90, 94. David Wells also echoes the misgivings of many in the evangelical movement about mysticism, and aspects of apophatic theology: 'People who are attracted to mysticism usually assume that what is hidden in God is other than what is revealed, or that it is deeper or more interesting or spiritually nourishing.' ibid., 132. He nonetheless makes the valid point that in the New Testament 'mystery' is typically associated with what is revealed and proclaimed, never with what is obscure and unknown. The

difficulty here is that we are slow on the uptake as to what is being revealed because of our blindness, hardness of heart, etc. which is that to which the catholic (in its broadest sense) traditions of spirituality are responding.

[10] Belden C. Lane, *The Solace of Fierce Landscapes* (New York: OUP, 1998), 53 NB: Westminster Catechism: 'Man's chief end is to glorify God, and to enjoy him for ever'.

[11] Alexander Schmemann, *Of Water and the Spirit* (New York: St Vladimir's Seminary Press, 1974), 107.

[12] Heather Ward, *Streams in Dry Land (Exploring Prayer)* (Washington DC: Eagle, 1993), 67.

[13] David Dales, *Glory* (Norwich: Canterbury Press, 2003), 61.

[14] St Bernard, *Serm. de divers*, 42. PL183, col.62AB quoted in Aelred Squire, *Asking the Fathers* (London & Norwich: SPCK, 1973), 31.

Chapter IV. The Unknowing of Faith

[1] Evagrius of Pontus, *Patrologia Graeca* 40:1275C, quoted in Bishop Kallistos Ware, *The Orthodox Way* (New York: SVS Press 1996), 11.

[2] Karen Armstrong, *The Case for God* (London: The Bodley Head, 2009), 124.

[3] *The Festal Menaion*, 291. quoted in Ware, ibid., 86.

[4] Neville Ward, *The Following Plough* (London: Epworth Press, 1978), 113.

[5] *Denys the Areopagite* is a pseudonym for an unknown Greek author who lived at the dawn of the sixth century. His *nom de plume* was culled from the reference to Dionysius (Denys) in the Book of Acts, rather in the way a blockbuster author today might choose to purloin a more racy name to market his mystery stories. (Dionysius was converted by Paul's preaching at the Areopagus in Athens).

[6] Literally *the negative way*, or better *the way of negation* where God is described by what God is not.

[7] See Exodus 24:15–18.

[8] Hilary Alfeyev, *The Mystery of Faith* (London & Oxford: DLT, 2002), 25–7.

[9] Vladimir Lossky, *The Mystical Theology of the Eastern Church* (Cambridge & London: James Clarke, 1957), 42.

[10] Matthew Fox OP, 'Eckhart, Meister' *A Dictionary of Christian Spirituality* (SCM, 1983), 123–5.

[11] St Anselm, *Monoologion, lxv*, quoted in Henri de Lubac, *The Discovery of God* (London & Oxford: DLT, 1960), 121–2.

[12] Henri de Lubac, *op. cit.*, 121–2.

[13] *The Cloud of Unknowing* (London: Penguin, 1961), 137.

[14] Kieran Kavanaugh, ed., St John of the Cross, *Collected Works* (Washington DC: ICS Publications, 1991), 126, 144.

[15] Lossky, *op. cit.*, 42.

[16] Lossky, *op. cit.*, 43.

[17] St Gregory the Theologian, *Dogmatic Poems* 1,1,29 trans. Phillip Schaff in *Cyril of Jerusalem, Gregory Nazianzen*, Nicene and Post-Nicene Fathers Series II, Vol. 7 (Grand Rapids, MI: Christian Classics Ethereal Library, 2009).

[18] St Augustine, *Confessions* Book 1, trans. Sir Tobie Matthew, KT, rev. Dom Roger Hudleston OSB (London & Glasgow: Fontana, 1963), 33.

[19] St Augustine, ibid., Book 3, 79. (Literal translation: 'But thou wast more interior to me than the innermost part of my soul').

[20] John Donne, 'Sermon CXLVI 29 February, 1627' *The Oxford Edition of the Sermons of John Donne, Vol. 5: Sermons Preached at Lincoln's Inn, 1620–1623*, ed. Katrin Ettenhuber (Oxford: OUP, 2015). Available online at www.biblestudytools.com/classica/the-works-of-john-donne-vol-5/sermon-cxlvi.html

Chapter V. Parting Well Made

[1] Meister Eckhart, Sermon, *Qui audit* me, quoted in Wolfgang Struve and George Wald, *Homo Mysticus: Three Lectures* (Washington DC: University Press of America, 2014), 39. Eckhart was a German Dominican mystic c. 1260–1327.

[2] R. S. Thomas, *Via Negativa: Later Poems* (London: Macmillan, 1983), 23.

[3] Carlo Carretto, *Letters From the Desert* (London: DLT, 1972), 14–16.

[4] 'Spiritual Canticle' stanzas 14 & 15 in *Collected Works of St John of the Cross*, trans. Kieran Kavanaugh OCD and Otilio Rodriguez OCD (Washington DC: ICS Publications, 1991), 473.

[5] Werner Pelz, 'A New Reformation—Beyond Theology', *Sermons from Great St Mary's* (London & Glasgow: Fontana, 1968).

[6] David Jasper, *The Sacred Desert* (Oxford: Blackwell, 2004), 11. See also: Palladius *The Lausiac History* transl. R. T. Meyer (Westminster Md: Newman Press, 1964), 110.

[7] André Louf, *Teach us to Pray*, New Edition (London: DLT, 1991).

Chapter VI. Living with Absurdity

[1] Tomáŝ Halík, *Night of the Confessor* (New York: Image Books, 2012), 27.

[2] See T. S. Eliot, *Four Quartets,* 'The Dry Salvages' in *Collected Poems 1909–1962* (London: Faber, 1974), 208.

[3] *Common Worship: Daily Prayer,* Evening Prayer for Advent (London: The Archbishops' Council, 2002), 179.

[4] Matthew 13:1–9; Mark 4:1–9; Luke 8:4–8.

[5] For Werner Pelz, see note 7, Chapter 3. Archbishop Rowan Williams has commented on 'the eloquence and freshness of the Pelzes remarkable book' (in *Anglican Identities* (London: DLT, 2014), 113). '*God is no More* is a book', suggests Williams, 'contemporaneous with John Robinson's *Honest to God* [(London: SCM Press, 1963)], but which nonetheless has more a substantial edge other than "appealing to the believer's moral intensity". Here the words of Jesus make possible a summons to "a re-imagining of yourself."' (Ibid., 114).

[6] *Yeshua,* the Hebrew form of the Greek *Ιησοΰς* (Jesus), would technically be rendered *Joshua* in English translations, thus maintaining the association with his namesake, before whose breath walls had crumbled, too. (See Lotte and Werner Pelz, *True Deceivers* (London: Collins, 1966), 43).

[7] These last two paragraphs are very much fashioned around the quixotic style of Werner Pelz's unfolding of the parables in *True Deceivers,* 220–45; also see *God is no More* Werner and Lotte Pelz (London: Victor Gollanz 1964), 54f, 84f.

[8] Vincent Donovan, *Christianity Rediscovered* (London: SCM Press, 1982), vii.

[9] Salley Vickers, *Mr. Golightly's Holiday* (New York: Harper Perennial, 2003), 157–8.

[10] Cyprian Smith OSB, *The Way of Paradox* (London: DLT, 2004), 73–4

[11] Harry Williams CR, *True Resurrection* (London: Mitchell Beazley, 1972), ix.

[12] Carlo Carretto, *Letters from the Desert* (London: DLT, 1972).

[13] Alan Ecclestone, *Yes to God* (London: DLT, 1975), 124.

[14] See Christopher Scott, 'The Uncertainty of Faith' *The Month* (October 1986), 270.

[15] Charles de Foucauld, *Letter to Mgr Caron,* quoted in Andrew Louth *The wilderness of God* (London: DLT, 1991), 13.

[16] Religious Orders for the *Little Brothers* and the *Little Sisters* were founded in the 1930s in Algeria, inspired by the life and writings of Charles de Foucauld. They remain essentially contemplative communities, with a presence in small hermitages in many of the poorest cities in the world, yet integrated with the local people.

[17] See Genesis 22:1–19.

[18] Herbert McCabe, *God, Christ and Us* (London & New York: Continuum, 2003), 35–40.

[19] Ibid., 40.

[20] See Isaiah 6:9–11 and Mark 4:11–12.

Chapter VII. The Imagination of our Hearts

[1] Marilynne Robinson, 'Imagination and Community' from *When I was a Child I Read Books* (London: Virago, 2012), 26.

[2] Peter Mullen, *The New Babel* (London: SPCK, 1987) See pp.42f for comparison of religious and scientific 'vocabulary'. 'Frail children of dust' from the hymn 'O worship the King' Robert Grant 1797–1838.

[3] *On What Cannot Be Said: Apophatic discourses in Philosophy, Religion, Literature and the Arts,* Ed. with Theoretical and Critical Essays by William Franke, 2 vols (Notre Dame: Notre Dame Press, 2007).

[4] Robinson, *op. cit.*, 19.

[5] Robinson, *op. cit.*, 19.

[6] Werner Pelz, '"The Emperor's New Clothes" or in defence of Dulcinea', 27 February 1996, *Sermons from Great St Mary's* (London & Glasgow: Fontana, 1968), 99.

[7] Jonathan Robinson, *The Mass and Modernity* (San Francisco: Ignatius Press, 2005), 262.

[8] Edward Henderson, Austin Farrer, 'The Sacramental Imagination' in *C. S. Lewis and Friends* (London: SPCK, 2011), 36. See also Austin Farrer, *The Crown of the Year* (Westminster: Dacre Press, 1952), 58.

[9] Farrer, *op. cit.*, 58

[10] From the Easter Proclamation or *Exsultet*, sung when in the darkened church the newly lit Easter Candle is placed in the midst of the people at the Vigil Service of Easter Day.

[11] David Wells, *Above All Earthly Powers: Christ in a Postmodern World* (Leicester: Inter-Varsity Press, 2005), 230.

[12] Metropolitan Anthony Bloom quoted by Jacob Needleman in *Lost Christianity* (Shaftesbury: Element Books, 1990), 34.

[13] For more information, see Edward Norman, *The House of God* (London: Thames and Hudson, 1990), 120, 123.

[14] Andrew Louth, *Eastern Orthodox Theology* (London: SPCK, 2013), 1.

[15] Wells, *op. cit.*, 203.

[16] Wells, *op. cit.*, 203–4.

[17] Wells, *op. cit.*, 206.

Chapter VIII. Actual Participation

[1] A. F. Dobbie-Bateman, *St Seraphim of Sarov: Concerning the aim of the Christian Life* (London: SPCK, 1936) 56, 58.

[2] Matt. 6:7.

[3] Laurence Hemming, *Worship as a Revelation* (London: Burns & Oates, 2008), 12.

[4] Hemming, ibid., 10.

[5] Fr. Gregory CSWG, Talk at Associates Conference in 1985 on *The Associates Manual, Eucharistic Living The Community of the Servants of the Will of God.* (Crawley Down: CSWG, 1984), 14.

[6] Hemming, ibid., 35.

[7] Fr Gregory CSWG, *The Holy Eucharist* (Crawley Down: CSWG, 1982) Introduction.

[8] Dom Alcuin Reid, 'Review of Laurence Paul Hemming, *The Past Present and Future of Catholic Liturgy*' in *The Catholic Herald*, 11 July 2008.

[9] Hemming, ibid., 31.

[10] William Barlow, *Intent Only on Life* (London: Collins, 1990), 125–36.

[11] *Parousia*: literally 'presence' or 'arrival'. A reference to the future return of Christ in glory.

[12] Fr Gregory, *op.cit.*, 14

Chapter IX. Worship as Revelation

[1] Hagia Sophia: this basilica was built in AD 573 as the seat of the Patriarch of Constantinople (now Istanbul). In 1453 it was converted into an Ottoman mosque. In 1931 it was secularised, and re-opened as a museum in 1935.

[2] Timothy Ware, *The Orthodox Church* (London: Penguin 1993), 264.

[3] Graham Greene, *Monsignor Quixote* (London: Penguin, 1983), 51.

[4] Fr George Rutler, Homily 18 May 2008 https://stmichaelnyc.org/documents/2017/3/2008-05-18.MP3

[5] Peter Mullen, *A Partial Vision: English Christianity and the Great Betrayal* (London: Watch House, 2010), 24.

[6] Book of Common Prayer: At Morning Prayer, *Quicunque Vult.*

[7] Evagrius of Pontus, *Patrologica Graeca* quoted in Ware, *op.cit.*

[8] C. S. Lewis, *The Lion, the Witch and the Wardrobe* (London: Harper-Collins, 1998).

[9] Brian Sibley, *The Land of Narnia* (London: Collins Lions, 1989), 90.

[10] Lesslie Newbigin, *Truth to tell: The Gospel as Public Truth* (Grand Rapids MI: Wm. B. Eerdmans, 1991), 10.

[11] This painting by Piero della Franscesca dates from 1460, and now resides in the artist's hometown of San Sepolcro in Italy at the Civico Museo. Comment on the sleeping soldiers from David McLaurin, 'Imagining the unimaginable' *Catholic Herald*, Easter Supplement 2008.

[12] Book of Common Prayer: Collects for Seasons of the Year: 'Easter Day'.

[13] Book of Common Prayer: The Easter Vigil in the Holy Night, 'The Easter Proclamation'.

[14] Fr. John Hunwicke, 'Easter apophatically', Liturgical Notes Blog, 25 April 2011. http://liturgicalnotes.blogspot.com/.

Epilogue

[1] Alexander Schmemann, *The world as sacrament* (London: DLT, 1966), 136.

[2] Andrew Miller, *Ingenious Pain* (London: Sceptre 1997), 214.

3 Kenneth Leech, *Spirituality and Pastoral Care* (London: Sheldon Press, 1986), 110.

[4] St Gregory of Nyssa, *The Life of Moses ii: Classics of Western Spirituality* (New Jersey: Paulist Press, 1978), 94–5.